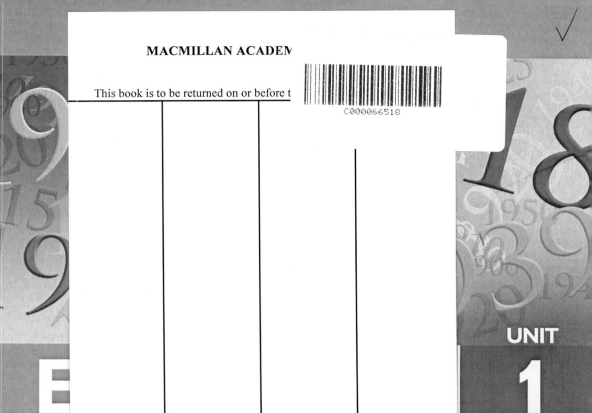

UNIT

1

E

History

The Collapse of the Liberal State and the Triumph of Fascism in Italy, 1896–1943 (Option E3/F3)

Derrick Murphy

Philip Allan Updates, an imprint of Hodder Education, an Hachette UK company, Market Place, Deddington, Oxfordshire OX15 0SE

Orders

Bookpoint Ltd, 130 Milton Park, Abingdon, Oxfordshire, OX14 4SB
tel: 01235 827827
fax: 01235 400401
e-mail: education@bookpoint.co.uk
Lines are open 9.00 a.m.–5.00 p.m., Monday to Saturday, with a 24-hour message answering service. You can also order through the Philip Allan Updates website: www.philipallan.co.uk

© Philip Allan Updates 2009

ISBN 978-0-340-99042-1

First printed 2009
Impression number 5 4 3
Year 2014 2013 2012

This guide has been written specifically to support students preparing for the Edexcel AS History Unit 1 examination. The content has been neither approved nor endorsed by Edexcel and remains the sole responsibility of the author.

Typeset by Phoenix Photosetting, Chatham, Kent
Printed by CPI Group (UK) Croydon, CR0 4YY

Hachette UK's policy is to use papers that are natural, renewable and recyclable products and made from wood grown in sustainable forests. The logging and manufacturing processes are expected to conform to the environmental regulations of the country of origin.

P01465

Contents

Introduction

■ ■ ■

Content Guidance

■ ■ ■

Questions and Answers

Introduction

Aims of the unit

Unit 1 is worth 25% of the A-level course (50% of the AS). It requires knowledge of the topic and the ability to explain historical events and assess their significance in a wider context. There are no sources on the exam paper, so source skills are unnecessary.

Questions require you to provide clear information that directly answers the question. In addition, examiners are looking for detailed and precise supporting evidence and examples to demonstrate that your statements are accurate. These examples need to be linked clearly to your argument.

You will have 40 minutes to write an answer to each question in the examination. In this time it is difficult to address every issue of some relevance to the question. Therefore, examiners will award full marks for answers that deal adequately, and in detail, with most of the central issues.

The Collapse of the Liberal State and the Triumph of Fascism in Italy, 1896–1943 is Option E3 of Paper 6HI01/E (or Option F3 of Paper 6HI01/F), The Expansion and Challenge of Nationalism. You need to be prepared for at least two topics from Option E (or F) and in the exam you will be required to answer questions relating to two different topics. This book deals exclusively with Option E3/F3.

The examination paper

The exam paper has seven topics, and you are required to answer questions on two of these topics. Each topic contains two questions and you can choose only one of these questions. The format of the topic questions in a typical examination paper is as follows:

> **6HI01/E — The Expansion and Challenge of Nationalism**
>
> **Answer TWO questions: ONE question on each of the TWO topics for which you have been prepared. You may only answer ONE question on each topic.**
>
> **E3 — The Collapse of the Liberal State and the Triumph of Fascism in Italy, 1896–1943**
>
> **EITHER**
>
> 9. How far was Mussolini able to create a dictatorship in Italy by 1940? **(Total: 30 marks)**
>
> **OR**
>
> 10. Why did Mussolini fall from power by July 1943? **(Total: 30 marks)**

Examinable skills

A total of 60 marks are available for Unit 1. Marks will be awarded for demonstrating the following skills:

- focusing on the requirements of the question, such as the topic, the period specified and the 'key concept'
- remembering, choosing and using historical knowledge
- analysing, explaining and reaching a judgement
- showing links between the key factors of your explanation

Focusing on the requirements of the question

Read the question carefully to ensure that you have noted the topic, the period and the key concept that is being addressed. One of the following concepts will be addressed by each question: causation, consequence, continuity, chance and significance.

Consider the following question:

Why did Mussolini become Italian prime minister in October 1922?
The topic is *the rise of Mussolini*, the period is *1919–22* and the key concept is causation — *explaining why Mussolini became prime minister.*

Remembering, choosing and using historical knowledge

When you have established what the question requires, you must decide which aspects of your own knowledge are relevant. Examiners are looking for an answer that covers between four and six factors. Next you must arrange these factors in a logical order to create a plan for your answer.

Once your structure is in place, you must develop it using specific examples. Try to ensure that your examples are detailed. You should include relevant dates; names of people, places, institutions and events; statistics and appropriate technical vocabulary. Examiners will reward both range and depth of knowledge.

Analysing, explaining and reaching a judgement

Telling the story of an event will not score well. It is expected that your answer will be arranged thematically, addressing different factors in turn.

Your key factors and supporting examples must be explicitly linked back to the question: that is to say, you must show how these details relate to or illustrate the argument that you are making. It is good practice to make these links at the end of each paragraph. It is also important that your essay reaches a clear judgement.

Showing links between the key factors of your explanation

In order to achieve the highest marks, you must highlight links between the factors that you have selected. This could mean demonstrating the relative importance of the different factors, or showing how the factors were dependent on each other.

Level descriptors

Answers are normally marked according to the five levels listed in the table below.

Level	Mark	Descriptor
1	1–6	Candidates produce mostly simple statements. These are supported by limited factual material which has some accuracy and relevance, although not directed at the focus of the question. The material is mostly generalised. There are few, if any, links between the simple statements. The writing may have limited coherence and is generally comprehensible, but passages lack both clarity and organisation. The skills needed to produce effective writing are not normally present. Frequent syntactical and/or spelling errors are likely to be present.
2	7–12	Candidates produce a series of simple statements supported by some mostly accurate and relevant factual material. The analytical focus is mostly implicit and there are likely to be only limited links between the simple statements. Material is unlikely to be developed very far. The writing has some coherence and is generally comprehensible, but passages lack both clarity and organisation. Some of the skills needed to produce effective writing are present. Frequent syntactical and/or spelling errors are likely to be present.
3	13–18	Candidates' answers attempt analysis and show some understanding of the focus of the question. However, they include material that either is descriptive, and thus only implicitly relevant to the question's focus, or which strays from that focus. Factual material will be accurate but it may lack depth and/or relevance in places. The writing is coherent in places but there are likely to be passages that lack clarity and/or proper organisation. Only some of the skills needed to produce convincing extended writing are likely to be present. Syntactical and/or spelling errors are likely to be present.
4	19–24	Candidates offer an analytical response that relates well to the focus of the question and shows some understanding of the key issues contained in it. The analysis is supported by accurate factual material which is mostly relevant to the question asked. The selection of material may lack balance in places. The answer shows some degree of direction and control but these attributes may not be sustained throughout the answer. The candidate demonstrates the skills needed to produce convincing extended writing but there may be passages that lack clarity or coherence. The answer is likely to include some syntactical and/or spelling errors.
5	25–30	Candidates offer an analytical response that directly addresses the focus of the question and demonstrates explicit understanding of the key issues contained in it. It is broadly balanced in its treatment of these key issues. The analysis is supported by accurate, relevant and appropriately selected factual material that demonstrates some range and depth. The exposition is controlled and the deployment logical. Some syntactical and/or spelling errors may be found but the writing is coherent overall. The skills required to produce convincing extended writing are in place.

How to use this guide

First, make sure that you understand the layout of the examination paper, the pattern of the marks and the types of question asked, all of which are explained above. Study the outline of the content required, which is given in the Content Guidance section. Try to:

- master the vocabulary and concepts given there
- establish clearly the important individuals and institutions which shaped the events of these years
- assess the extent of change between 1896 and 1943

The most important part of the guide is the Questions and Answers section, which provides five examples of the kinds of question that you will be asked. It is important to work through these, studying the two sets of sample answers provided and the examiner's comments. The first answer to each question is an A-grade response which, although not perfect, gives a good idea of what is required. The purpose of the second answer is to illustrate some of the common errors made by students.

Content
Guidance

The specification for Option E3/F3 of Unit 1 is divided into four key issues:

- Weaknesses of the political system and attempts to stabilise it from 1903 under Giolitti; social discontent and political disorder, 1896–1912.
- The impact of the First World War on Italy and its impact on the Liberal state, 1918–23: Mussolini and the message and appeal of Fascism, 1919–22.
- Power and control in Fascist Italy: propaganda; terror; the PNF (*Partito Nazionale Fascista*); the relationship of the regime with the Church and the old elites.
- Building the new Roman Empire: Abyssinia, Spain and Italy's diplomatic and military preparations for war, 1933–41.

To help you understand what will be required for this AS unit, the content has been broken down into sections. Where appropriate, the section ends with an extended explanation of key terms and personalities.

Outline of topics

Italy in 1896: a survey

The Italian political system

The problem of the Papacy

Economic problems

Cultural variations

Italy's position in international affairs

1896–1914: attempts to stabilise the Liberal state

Giolitti's government and the reform of the political system

Italian foreign policy, 1890–1915

Italy on the eve of the First World War

The impact of the First World War on Italy

The decision to enter the war

The Italian front, 1915–18

The impact of the war on Italy

The postwar economic and political crisis

The impact of the peace treaties on Italy

Postwar economic problems

Political problems

The rise of Fascism to power by 1922

Mussolini's background

The creation of the Fascist Party

How did the Fascists gain support?

How did Mussolini become prime minister?

1922–25: consolidation of power

The Catholic Church

Fascist relations with other political parties

The Acerbo Law, July 1923

The Matteotti Affair and the Aventine Secession

The creation of the Fascist state

The corporate state

Economic policies
- The return to economic protectionism and quota 90
- Battles for Grain and Births

Relations with the king and the Catholic Church
- King Victor Emmanuel
- The Catholic Church

Propaganda, youth and social control
- The cult of Il Duce
- Education and youth
- Leisure and sport
- The role of women

The police state
- What was Fascism?
- Who supported Fascism?
- How authoritarian was Fascist Italy?

Mussolini's foreign policy: 1922–43

Mussolini's aims

The Lausanne Conference, Fiume and Corfu

Extending influence in the Adriatic region

The Abyssinian War, 1935–36

The Spanish Civil War, 1936–39

Brutal friendship: relations with Germany, 1933–39

The impact of the Second World War on Italy

The military situation, 1940–43

The home front

Italy in 1896: a survey

In 1896, Italy had been a united country for only 35 years, following a long history of political and economic disunity. For over 1,000 years since the collapse of the Roman empire, the Italian peninsula had been divided into a number of states. However, between 1859 and 1861 the Italians experienced a series of wars of unification. During these wars, mainly with French help, the Italian state of **Piedmont-Sardinia** was able to acquire most of northern and central Italy. In southern Italy, the Italian nationalist Giuseppe Garibaldi conquered the independent kingdom of Naples and Sicily and handed the territory to the king of Piedmont-Sardinia. Consequently, Italy had become a united kingdom in a very short period. In 1866, Venetia was acquired from the Austrian empire and, in 1870, Rome was annexed. The speed of this unification process, known as *Il Risorgimento* (The Resurrection), would create major problems for the new Italian state.

The Italian political system

The head of state was a monarch, the former king of Piedmont-Sardinia. In 1896, the king was Umberto I, who ruled from 1878 to 1900, when he was assassinated by an anarchist. Italy was a constitutional monarchy, governed by *Il Statuto*, the Piedmontese constitution of 1849. The king could appoint and dismiss the prime minister and other members of the government. However, a government could survive only if it commanded a majority of seats in the lower house of parliament. In 1896, Italy was not a democratic state. The right to vote was limited to the rich. Only in 1911 was **universal manhood suffrage** introduced. As a result, parliament was dominated by landowners, businessmen and members of the professional classes. By 1896, in a bid to create an element of stability between successive governments, the *transformiso* system had been developed. This meant that governments were decided more by ministers and members of parliament than the electorate and political parties. Such a system was criticised as corrupt, sustaining government stability at the expense of real political debate on government policy.

The problem of the Papacy

A major problem facing the new Italian state was the position of the **Papacy**. Italy was an overwhelmingly Catholic country. Until 1861, **the Pope** ruled a large area of central Italy called the **Papal States**. However, by 1861 all the Papal States except Rome had been absorbed into the new kingdom of Italy. From 1870, Rome became part of Italy and its new capital. The Pope had been transformed from the position of independent ruler to that of Italian citizen. In 1871, the Law of Guarantees gave the Pope many of the rights of an independent ruler, such as granting full diplomatic status to foreign envoys to the Vatican. However, it did not give the Pope complete independence. As a result, Pope Pius IX (1846–78) made known his opposition to the new liberal kingdom of Italy. In 1871 he issued a decree, *Non Expedit* (Not expedient), where he ruled that it was unwise for Catholics to vote in national elections. However, many Catholics ignored this advice and by 1896 a large number had become members of parliament. In 1874 the Pope created *Opera dei Congressi* (congressional work) to coordinate Catholic activity in education and social work. Twenty years later, Italy had a widespread network of Catholic organisations under its control. Liberal politicians saw this as a major threat to their power and influence.

Economic problems

Italy possessed a varied economy. In the north, industry and commerce had been developed in the Middle Ages. Turin and Milan were important industrial cities engaged in textile production and engineering, while Genoa and Venice were major European seaports. However, the further south one travelled, the more agricultural and economically primitive Italy became. Most Italians in 1896 worked in agriculture. In the south, in the former kingdom of Naples and Sicily, many people were engaged in subsistence farming. The majority of farm workers were illiterate. By the twentieth century, this area became known as the Mezzogiorno. Conditions were made worse by a tariff war with France between 1881 and 1888, which adversely affected the south. The poor economic conditions led to mass emigration, particularly from southern Italy. Initially Italians emigrated to France or Germany, but by 1896, the vast majority of these emigrants were going to the New World. Thousands went to Argentina, but the majority ended up in the USA.

Even with mass emigration resulting in a smaller population to feed, Italy remained an economically backward country. Attempts were made by successive governments to improve matters. The railway network was extended into the Mezzogiorno. However, successive 'liberal' governments were committed to low taxation and limited government involvement in economic affairs and thus the practical help provided was limited.

However, in 1896 a European-wide economic depression that had lasted since 1873 came to an end. Italy, and northern Italy in particular, went through a period of major industrial and economic growth from 1896 to 1915. With this growth came a rise in the number of industrial workers who were attracted to Socialist ideas, such as a much more positive role for the state in the provision of social welfare.

Cultural variations

Owing to the long history of political disunity and economic diversity, Italy possessed a wide variety of regional differences. Even today, Italians talk of *campanilismo* (strong regional identity). Until the nineteenth century, Italy comprised a number of competing states. City states such as Genoa, Venice, Florence and Siena had gone to war with each other in the past. As a result, most Italians saw themselves as Florentines or Venetians first and Italians second.

Modern Italian developed from the regional language of Tuscany. Other parts of Italy retained strong local dialects. With much of the poor peasant population being illiterate in 1896, many Italians found it difficult to communicate with each other. Italian, in its modern written and spoken form, was the preserve of the middle and upper classes.

The economic diversity of Italy also accentuated differences. The cities of Turin, Milan and Venice had more in common with cities in France and Germany than with the rest of Italy. In the economically backward island of Sicily, organised crime, controlled by the Mafia, was a constant feature of everyday life. The Mafia was not a unified body but comprised a number of competing extended family groups. As a result, the maintenance of law and order and effective government in Sicily was adversely affected. Other organisations similar to the Mafia also existed in the southern Italian provinces of Basilicata, Campania and Puglia.

Italy's position in international affairs

In 1896, European affairs were dominated by the five **great powers** of Germany, Russia, Britain, Austria-Hungary and France. Italy aspired to be regarded as a great power, but it lacked the military and economic strength to do so. However, this did not mean Italy did not play an important part in European affairs. In 1882, it formed the Triple Alliance with Germany and Austria-Hungary. This was a secret military alliance, mainly aimed against France and Russia. It was renewed by Italy every 3 years until 1914.

Like most of the great powers, Italy also wished to develop an overseas colonial empire. Until 1881, Italian politicians had hoped to acquire the Turkish province of Tunis in North Africa, only to be pipped to the post by France, which took control of the province instead. This was a major factor behind Italy's decision to join the Triple Alliance. However, by 1896, Italy had acquired colonial control over Eritrea on the Red Sea and Somaliland, both in east Africa. In that year, it then attempted to extend its colonial control over east Africa with the acquisition of the ancient kingdom of Abyssinia (modern-day Ethiopia), only to suffer a major military defeat at the hands of the Abyssinian army at the Battle of Adowa. This was the only time in the nineteenth century that a European state was defeated by an African state in war. The resulting political humiliation led to the resignation of the prime minister, **Francesco Crispi**, and his government. Although the Battle of Adowa was a national humiliation, it did not end Italy's desire to acquire an overseas empire.

Glossary

Piedmont-Sardinia: a kingdom of northwest Italy comprising the cities of Turin, Genoa and the island of Sardinia. It was the only Italian state completely free from Austrian influence after the Napoleonic Wars.

universal male suffrage: the right to vote for all adult men.

Papacy: the rule of the Pope.

the Pope: the leader of the Roman Catholic Church. He is based in the Vatican City in Rome and is chosen from among the senior churchmen of the Catholic Church, called cardinals. From the 1520s until 1978, all popes were Italian.

Papal States: the area of central Italy ruled by the Pope. Until 1860, it comprised the Romagna, Umbria, the Marches and Rome.

great powers: the five major powers of Europe in the period 1815–1918. Great powers were characterised by their military strength.

Key figure

Francesco Crispi (1819–1901): Crispi was a Liberal all his life. He participated in the Liberal revolt against the king of Naples in 1848. He was an important participator in Giuseppe Garibaldi's invasion of Sicily in 1860, which was one of the most critical episodes in the unification of Italy. He was minister of the interior 1876–77 and prime minister 1887–90 and again 1893–96. He was pro-German and anti-French in his foreign policy and supported the Triple Alliance.

1896–1914: attempts to stabilise the Liberal state

Giolitti's government and the reform of the political system

Between 1896 and 1914, the Liberal state in Italy faced a variety of problems. Economic backwardness and the European economic depression had caused widespread social distress. This was alleviated in part by mass emigration, but the country still faced riots and strikes. In 1898, following a rise in food prices, the workers of Milan rioted. The government introduced martial law and, in a clash between the army and rioters, 100 rioters were killed and another 400 wounded. The social conditions, combined with industrial development, gave rise to the growth of the Italian Socialist Party, which advocated major political and social change.

Another challenge to the Liberal state was the Catholic Church, the Pope never having reconciled himself to the loss of his political independence in 1870. In addition, Du Rudini — the prime minister from 1896 to 1898 — regarded Catholic social organisations across Italy as agents of the Pope and attempted to repress them.

Finally, the political system lacked support from the vast majority of Italians. Widely regarded as corrupt, the Liberal politicians did not have the political power and authority to unite the country. In 1882, an electoral law was passed which gave the vote to all literate Italian males. However, these constituted less than 50% of the adult male population. If Italy was to progress as a major European power, these problems had to be addressed.

The most influential Italian politician from 1896 to 1914 was **Giovanni Giolitti**. He served first as a minister in a number of governments, most notably as minister of the interior in the 1899–1903 government, before becoming prime minister from 1903–1905, 1906–09 and 1911–14.

Giolitti's attempts to reform and modernise Italy, which began long before his appointment as prime minister, are known as Giolittism. In 1893, he helped create the Bank of Italy, which put an end to the financial instability associated with the banking system. He abandoned the repressive policies of his predecessors, trying instead to broaden the base of the Liberal state by encompassing workers and Catholics.

In 1902, the Supreme Council of Labour was created, which allowed trade unions a role in the preparation of social legislation. Giolitti also introduced laws banning child labour and limiting the hours of work for women. In 1901, he allowed unions of agricultural labourers to organise and strike. Unfortunately, many of Giolitti's reforms were attacked by both right and left. Landowners thought he was going too far, while trade unions and Socialists believed he had not been radical enough.

With regard to the Catholics, Giolitti benefited from the Pope's concern about the rise of socialism. Regarding this as anti-Catholic, he was forced to relax his opposition to the Italian state. Many Catholics had already defied papal advice by voting and participating in elections, and in 1909, the Pope allowed Catholics to stand for parliament, although many Catholics had previously ignored the Pope. Relying on Catholic and moderate support, Giolitti was able to become prime minister in 1909 and again in 1911.

In a further effort to broaden support, in his last administration before the First World War, Giolitti introduced universal male suffrage — a move associated with promises to the Socialists that he would introduce social insurance for workers and old age pensions. However, instead of fulfilling these promises, Giolitti invaded the Turkish province of Libya in a bid to win nationalist support for his regime. In the Italian-Turkish War of 1911–12, Italy gained Libya and the **Dodecanese islands** off Turkey for its empire. As a consequence, however, Giolitti lost Socialist support from 1911 and increasingly relied on Catholic and moderate backing.

Despite all his efforts, in the summer of 1914 — shortly before the outbreak of the First World War — Italy was plagued by growing social unrest in the form of demonstrations, riots and strikes. It would seem that Giolitti's attempts to unite the Italian population behind the Liberal state were failing.

Italian foreign policy, 1896–1915

The period from 1880 to 1914 was the 'Age of Imperialism'. During this time, European states established large colonial empires across the world, the largest being the British empire. By 1914, this covered one quarter of the world's surface and contained one third of the global population. The clearest manifestation of European imperialism was the Partition of Africa. In 1880, European occupation was restricted mainly to the coastal areas of the continent. By 1914, however, all of

Africa except for Liberia (under US protection) and Abyssinia was under European control.

Like other European states, Italy also wanted its 'place in the sun'. In the 1880s, successive Italian governments tried to establish a strong Italian presence in east Africa. In 1881, it hoped to acquire Tunis in north Africa, which instead fell under French control. In 1883, it acquired Eritrea as a colony, to be followed by Somaliland in 1885. In the 1890s, it attempted to acquire Abyssinia, but this plan came to an abrupt end with the Italian defeat at the Battle of Adowa in 1896.

Defeat at the hands of Abyssinia did not end the desire of Italian nationalists to develop an overseas empire, however. By 1911, France had extended its control over the north African coast, controlling Algeria and Morocco in addition to its previous acquisition of Tunis. Encouraged by this development, Giolitti's government decided to go to war with the Ottoman (Turkish) empire in September of the same year. Italian forces conquered the Ottoman province of Libya in North Africa after a brief war. In the subsequent peace treaty in October 1912, Italy acquired Libya and the Dodecanese Islands, in the Aegean Sea.

Another area of great interest in international affairs was the issue of the *Irredenta*. This referred to areas within Austria-Hungary which contained sizeable Italian-speaking populations. Nationalists wished to unite all Italians within the Italian state, and therefore regarded areas such as the Trentino and the city port of Trieste as places which should be joined with the rest of Italy. In several governments, a minister of the *Irredenta* areas was appointed. Other more extreme nationalists wished to acquire territories in Austria-Hungary that had been formerly part of the Italian states, such as Venice. They also had their sights on the Adriatic coast of Austria-Hungary, known as **Dalmatia**. Not surprisingly, these demands caused friction within the Triple Alliance, with two of the three members having such conflicting interests.

Successive Italian governments renewed the Triple Alliance every 3 years up to 1914. However, in 1902 the Zanardelli government concluded a secret alliance with France, which contradicted the terms of the Triple Alliance. The Triple Alliance continued to be renewed for another 12 years after this breach.

Italy on the eve of the First World War

During the period 1896–1914, Italy underwent major economic change. Economic growth over that period averaged 4% per year. In the 25 years before the outbreak of the First World War, national income rose by 50% and industrial production came to constitute 25% of total national output. Italy also played a major role in the early development of the motor car, with the Fiat car company being founded in Turin in 1899. However, much of the benefit of economic growth was centred in northern Italy. Government attempts to encourage similar growth in southern Italy foundered as a result of unskilled labour, poor communications and a lack of natural resources. Although it was possible to regard Italy as a rising industrial power, it was still far behind the great powers of Britain, France and Germany.

Economic growth also brought major social changes and a growing rift between rich and poor. When the First World War began in August 1914, Italy seemed to be on the verge of considerable social unrest, the summer of that year having seen an increase in strikes and demonstrations across the country. This was largely the result of a change in demographics: the rapid industrial growth had created a large working class in cities like Turin and Milan in north Italy, a group which was attracted to the Socialists, who demanded better living and working conditions for industrial workers. However, the potential social crisis came to an abrupt end with the outbreak of war.

At the same time, the Giolitti system of government was also facing a crisis. Giolitti's failure to deliver on his social reform programme of 1911 (due to his war with the Ottoman empire) had alienated the Socialists, and following an increase in the franchise (the right to vote), the number of Liberal deputies in parliament declined. In the 1913 general election — the first following the creation of universal male suffrage in 1911 — Giolitti returned as prime minister. However, he was now heavily dependent on Catholic support, which alienated his Liberal followers. As a result, his support split and Giolitti was forced to resign on 21 March 1914.

As the First World War began, the Italian political system seemed to be more divided and divisive than ever. The deep social and economic rifts were still unbridged. Socialists and trade unions demanded a more equitable distribution of wealth, while nationalists wanted Italy to be regarded as a great power with a large overseas empire. The creation of universal male suffrage in 1911 reduced the electoral base of the Liberals. Liberals hoped that the new voters would support them, but Liberal support tended to come from the middle classes. The new voters came from the working class and poor farmers. Catholics were divided over their view towards the Liberal state. Many Catholics voted and stood for parliament, but the Papacy still opposed the Italian state and Catholic social organisations operated in an atmosphere that brought them into conflict with Liberal governments.

Glossary

Dodecanese islands: Greek islands which include Rhodes and Kos.

Abyssinia: now known as Ethiopia.

Dalmatia: the eastern coastline of the Adriatic Sea, now in Slovenia and Croatia.

Key figure

Giovanni Giolitti (1842–1928): born in Piedmont-Sardinia and minister of finance under Crispi from 1889 to 1890. He was also the minister of the interior 1901–03 and prime minister 1903–05, 1906–09, 1911–14 and 1920–21.

The impact of the First World War on Italy

The decision to enter the war

In August 1914, Europe plunged into the First World War. Austria-Hungary was supported by its Triple Alliance ally Germany, while the French and Russians supported each other in line with the terms of the Franco-Russian Alliance of 1893. On 4 August 1914, Britain joined France and Russia in their war against Germany. What would Italy do? Under prime minister **Antonio Salandra**, Italy declared itself neutral. In defence of this position, the Italian government claimed that it had not been offered territory by Austria-Hungary when Austria-Hungary attacked Serbia. From August 1914 to May 1915, both the central powers (Germany and Austria-Hungary) and the Allied powers (France, Russia and Britain) tried to woo Italy into joining them. Following the Treaty of London, in which Britain and France offered Italy considerable territorial gains at the expense of Austria-Hungary if it would enter the war, prime minister Salandra joined the Allied powers in April 1915. Without consulting parliament, but after gaining the king's support, he declared war on Austria-Hungary on 23 May 1915.

> The Italian government on July 27th and 28th 1914, emphasised in clear and unmistakable language to Berlin and Vienna the question of the cession of the Italian provinces governed by Austria-Hungary and we declared that if we did not obtain adequate compensation, the Triple Alliance would have been irreparably broken. Austria-Hungary did not respond to our demands, which are first, the defence of Italianism, the greatest of our duties; secondly, a secure military frontier, replacing that which was imposed upon us in 1866, by which all the gates of Italy are open to our adversaries. These essential advantages were substantially denied us.
>
> Extract from Salandra's speech to the Italian parliament on 23 May 1915, announcing the reasons for Italy entering the First World War

The Italian front, 1915–18

Italy entered the First World War on a wave of nationalist enthusiasm. Its main opponent was Austria-Hungary. In May 1915, Austria-Hungary was fighting against Serbia and had suffered a series of defeats against Russia on the Eastern Front. However, early Italian optimism soon evaporated. Italy was not prepared to fight a major war against a great power: the economy was not geared towards war production and the army had little experience of fighting a war and was poorly led. In 1915–16, the Italians launched a number of offensives against the

Austro-Hungarian army. In the 11 battles of the Isonzo they gained little territory at great human cost, losing over 300,000 troops. In many ways, the Italian front resembled the Western front, in that it was virtually static.

The main event on the Italian front in the First World War was the Battle of Caporetto from 24 October to 17 November 1917. Following the collapse of the tsarist government in Russia, the Germans were able to transfer troops to the Italian front in support of their Austro-Hungarian allies. In the battle, the Austro-German forces inflicted a major defeat on the Italians, who retreated in disarray to the River Piave, 100 miles behind the lines. The city of Venice was threatened with capture and the Italians lost 265,000 prisoners of war. The complete collapse of the Italian front at this point was only prevented by the transfer of British and French troops from the Western front and a heroic Italian defence of the River Piave valley, in particular at Monte Grappa. This battle was a turning point in the Italian war effort. The commander-in-chief, Cardorna, was sacked by the government, as he was commander in the Battle of Caporetto, and replaced by General Armando Diaz. Diaz reorganised the supply and training of the army. In June 1918, the Italian army repulsed an Austro-German offensive on the Piave and in October, supported by British and French units, launched its own offensive which led to a breakthrough at the Battle of Vittorio-Veneto between 23 October and 3 November. By the end of this battle, the Austro-Hungarian government requested an armistice (ceasefire) and the war on the Italian front came to an end.

The impact of the war on Italy

The First World War had a profound impact on Italy. Although nationalists had welcomed Italy's entry into the war, this view was not shared by Socialists. The Socialist newspaper *Avanti!* (*Forward!*) was a major critic. Following the defeat by the Austro-German forces at the Battle of Caporetto, the Italian government looked for scapegoats and regarded the Socialists as 'the enemy within'. From 1917, the government clamped down on Socialist political activity. As a result, the war helped divide Italy more openly into rival political camps.

The experience of war also had lasting effects. Three million men served in the armed forces, of whom 650,000 were killed (Britain lost 750,000). Of the nearly 600,000 who became prisoners of war, 100,000 died in captivity. One of those who served and was wounded was the former editor of *Avanti!*, Benito Mussolini. His personal experience of combat transformed his political views. He ceased to be an anti-war Socialist and became a fervent Nationalist.

On the home front, parliament played a minor role in the governance of the country. Instead, through censorship and the economic direction of the war, the government operated almost like a dictatorship, particularly after Caporetto. The *Mobilitizione Industriale* (MI) was a group of industries that worked with the government in producing war material. In MI factories strikes were made illegal and work hours extended. Huge profits were made by companies such as Ansaldo, whose production and workforce increased tenfold during the war. At the same time, the war also resulted in food shortages and the cost of living (measured through the rate of inflation) rose by 300%. In order to finance military action, Italy had borrowed huge sums of money, mainly from the USA and Britain. The national debt rose from 16 billion lire in 1914 to 85 billion lire in 1919.

However, in November 1918, Italy was one of the victorious allies. The country's main opponent, Austria-Hungary, was not only defeated but, at the war's end, disintegrated into smaller ethnic states such as Austria, Czechoslovakia and Hungary. Yet the euphoria of November 1918 was short lived.

The postwar economic and political crisis

The impact of the peace treaties on Italy

The peace conference to decide the fate of Europe took place in Paris in 1919. Italy was regarded as one of the **Big Four** Allied powers, along with the USA, Britain and France. Russia left the war in March 1918 and was under Communist control. By 1919, the Communist government was fighting a bitter civil war and was not invited to the Paris Peace Conference.

Under the terms of the Treaty of London of May 1915, Italy was promised large parts of the Austro-Hungarian empire by the Allies. These included the Trentino, the port of Trieste and a large section of Austria-Hungary's Adriatic coast called Dalmatia. However, in the peace negotiations of 1919, Italy received far less territory. This was in part due to its poor military performance as an ally. Without British and French support, Italy could have been forced out of the war after Caporetto. Also the US president, Woodrow Wilson, supported the idea of national self-determination, whereby the political units of Europe should be based on ethnic unity. Most of Dalmatia was not Italian speaking, being made up of Slavic-speaking peoples such as Slovenes, Croats and Montenegrins. As a result, in the Treaty of St Germain, Italy received the Trentino, South Tyrol, Trieste and the Istrian peninsula. This was seen as a major national humiliation. Following the peace negotiations, the British prime minister, David Lloyd George, claimed in his memoirs that he heard the Italian prime minister, **Vittorio Emanuele Orlando**, crying over Italy's treatment.

To many Italians, the Paris peace treaties resulted in a 'mutilated victory'. Italy had fought for nearly 4 years and lost 650,000 soldiers but received little territorial gain. Nationalists were particularly appalled. One war hero, the aviator **Gabriele D'Annunzio**, took matters into his own hands. Outraged by the mutilated peace, in 1919, he and 2,000 followers occupied the port of Fiume (modern day Rijeka) on the Adriatic Sea, which had been promised to Italy in the Treaty of London in May 1915

Italy in 1920

but was withheld at the subsequent Paris Peace Conference. For 14 months, D'Annunzio occupied Fiume, until he was dislodged by the Italian armed forces, under severe pressure from Britain and France. In that time, D'Annunzio established an authoritarian regime in which rival social and economic organisations, such as employers and workers, were forced to work together in what became known as the corporate state. His followers wore black shirts and gave the ancient Roman salute, both of which were later copied by Mussolini for his Fascist supporters.

D'Annunzio's rule in Fiume highlighted a number of important issues. He proved that the Italian government had failed. He acquired land that Orlando had not succeeded in acquiring in Paris. Also, his 14-month rule showed that the Italian government was powerless to intervene and that the armed forces were reluctant to dislodge a person regarded by many Italians as a war hero. D'Annunzio's actions stood in marked contrast to the poor performance of Orlando and his government at Paris. His achievements and method of government in Fiume were not lost on Benito Mussolini.

Postwar economic problems

Like every other major combatant in the First World War, Italy faced a massive economic crisis at the end of the war. The conflict had completely disrupted international trade. All the combatants except the USA had amassed huge war debts that had to be repaid. Four pre-war empires had collapsed: Germany, Russia, Austria-Hungary and the Ottoman empire. New states appeared after the 1919 peace treaties such as Poland, Czechoslovakia and Yugoslavia.

Italy's economic crisis was of major proportions. At the end of the war, armaments production ceased, creating unemployment and a slowdown in economic growth, and the demobilisation of 2 million soldiers swelled the ranks of the unemployed. The war had radicalised the industrial workers, with membership of the Socialist Party rising from 50,000 in 1914 to nearly 200,000 in 1919. In the countryside, the war had led to tensions between landowners and agricultural labourers. Like the industrial workers, agricultural workers wanted to see major social and economic change after the war. The combination of the decline in the economy and rising unemployment helped create the conditions for a large-scale political crisis.

Political problems

The economic impact of war and the disappointing 'mutilated victory' discredited the Liberal state. Hundreds of thousands of Italians had died and the country faced major economic dislocation for scant reward. Dissatisfaction with the Liberals was shown in the first general election after the war on 16 November 1919. The Liberals received 904,000 votes (16.4% of the vote) and gained 96 seats in the lower house of parliament. In contrast, the Socialists won 1,800,000 votes (32.3% of the vote) and became the largest party with 156 seats. For the first time in the history of the Italian state, a Catholic party, the *Popolari*, fought the election. It gained 1 167,000 votes (20% of the vote) and became the second largest party with 150 seats. In the period following the election up to 1922, disillusion with the Liberal state continued to grow and a new type of mass politics developed. Soldiers, radicalised by their war experience and facing a bleak economic future, were attracted to political parties and groups which offered radical solutions to Italy's mounting problems.

Glossary

Big Four: the name given to the leaders of the main Allied powers. They were President Woodrow Wilson of the USA, Georges Clemenceau of France, David Lloyd George of the British empire and prime minister Vittorio Emanuele Orlando of Italy. Most of the major decisions were made by the first three politicians, also known as the Big Three.

Treaty of St Germain: the peace treaty between the Allies and Austria. A separate peace treaty, the Treaty of Trianon, was made with Hungary as the Austro-Hungarian empire had disintegrated by 1919.

Key figures

Antonio Salandra (1853–1931): prime minister from March 1914 to June 1916. A lawyer and right-wing Liberal, he had been a member of the Italian national parliament 1886–1928. He was the politician most responsible for Italy's entry into the First World War. After 1919, he attempted to form a coalition of Liberals and nationalists during Facta's government of February to October 1922. At this point, he supported the appointment of Mussolini as prime minister.

Vittorio Emanuele Orlando (1860–1952): born in Palermo, Sicily. He became prime minister in October 1917 after the Italian defeat in the Battle of Caporetto and led Italy to victory in the First World War. He became disillusioned with Italy's treatment at the Paris Peace Conference and resigned as a result in June 1919.

Gabriele D'Annunzio (1863–1938): a major poet and Italian war hero of the First World War. He was an aviator who was involved in the bombing of Vienna, the Austro-Hungarian capital. After the war, he became disillusioned with the peace settlement and supported direct, heroic political action. The main example of this was his occupation of Fiume (Rijeka) in 1919–20. His actions and method of rule were subsequently copied by Mussolini.

The rise of Fascism to power by 1922

Mussolini's background

In October 1922, Benito Mussolini became Italy's youngest prime minister of the twentieth century. He was also the longest serving, holding the office until July 1943. Mussolini created his own political movement and ideology called Fascism, which created a right-wing, nationalist dictatorship. Yet Mussolini's background suggested that he might follow a different direction. He was born on 29 July 1883 near the town of Forli in **the Romagna**, Central Italy. His father was a blacksmith who had strong Socialist views. His mother had been a school teacher and was a devout Catholic. Mussolini was named after Benito Juarez, a Mexican revolutionary of the mid-nineteenth century.

Although initially educated at a Catholic school, at the age of 11 years Mussolini was expelled for knifing a fellow pupil. As a young man, he spent time teaching and travelling. Between 1902 and 1904, he lived in Switzerland, where he worked as a manual labourer. However, he also began writing for Socialist newspapers, an occupation that would earn him a national reputation when he returned to Italy in 1906. In January 1910, he started his own Socialist newspaper, *La Lotta di Classe* (*The Class Struggle*), in his home region of the Romagna. In November 1912, Mussolini's career had a breakthrough when he was appointed editor of *Avanti!* (*Forward!*), the national Socialist newspaper. When the First World War broke out in Europe in August 1914, Mussolini's career as a Socialist journalist and politician seemed set to continue, especially in view of the fact that Italy remained neutral until May 1915 — a position supported by Socialists.

However, on 18 October 1914 Mussolini wrote an article for *Avanti!* supporting Italy's entry into the war on the Allied side. As a result of this article, Mussolini was expelled from the Italian Socialist Party (PSI) on 24 November 1914. Why did Mussolini make such a radical change in his political views? In many ways he acted like other European Socialists in France and Germany, who supported their own country's war efforts. He may also have been affected by his failure to win a seat in parliament in the 1913 general election. Following his expulsion from the Socialist Party, he set up his own newspaper, *Il Popolo d'Italia* (*The Italian People*), which supported entry into the war and had a strong nationalist content. In helping to create the newspaper, Mussolini received payments from the Allies, who were keen that the benefits of Italian entry into the war on the Allied side be put across to the Italian public.

Another life-changing development came when Mussolini was conscripted into the Italian army in August 1915. He spent time at the Front and was wounded in an accident involving a mortar in February 1917. He was invalided out of the army with the rank of corporal, the same rank as Adolf Hitler. Mussolini returned to civilian life and resumed his career as editor of *Il Popolo d'Italia*.

The political and economic crisis facing Italy after the First World War provided the background for Mussolini's rapid rise to power, as he was able to exploit these conditions for his own benefit.

The creation of the Fascist Party

In March 1919, Mussolini founded the *Fasci di Combattimento* (Combat Squads), a new political force. The party programme of 1919 advocated the abolition of the monarchy and the creation of a republic. It supported the decentralisation of government and the abolition of military conscription. In many ways, the party was left-wing and a rival to the Socialists, supporting the closure of all banks and the stock exchange, and wanting profit sharing between factory owners and their workers. The party was also anti-clerical; it wanted all lands owned by the Catholic Church to be seized by the Italian state. Mussolini also denounced the treatment of Italy at the **Paris Peace Conference of 1919–20** and hoped to win industrial workers and agricultural labourers away from the Socialists to his new party.

However, 1919 did not prove to be an auspicious year for the new Fascists. In the national elections of November that year, every Fascist candidate was defeated, including Mussolini. Instead, the elections resulted in success for the Socialist Party and the new Catholic party, the *Popolari*. Faced with electoral humiliation, however, Mussolini merely changed the party programme. The Fascists promptly became strongly Nationalist, dropping their opposition to both the monarchy and the Catholic Church. The period 1919–22 was a time of almost continual political, social and economic crisis and Mussolini exploited these conditions.

How did the Fascist Party gain support?

Italian prime ministers 1917–43		Period in office
Vittorio Orlando	October 1917–June 1919	1 year, 7 months
Francesco Nitti	June 1919–June 1920	1 year
Giovanni Giolitti	June 1920–July 1921	1 year, 1 month
Ivanoe Bonomi	July 1921–February 1922	7 months
Luigi Facta	February 1922–October 1922	8 months
Benito Mussolini	October 1922–July 1943	20 years, 9 months

From the end of 1919, Mussolini stressed two major aims for Fascism: it was strongly nationalist and anti-Socialist. Given the conditions of the time, both ideas struck a reassuring chord and quickly gained in popularity. In 1918, trade union membership stood at 250,000. By 1920 it had risen to 1.2 million. This rise occurred at a time of major economic crisis. The value of the Italian currency, the lira, had dropped dramatically after the end of the war: in March 1919, the lira was worth 30 lira to one British pound; by December 1920, it had fallen in value to 100 lire to the pound. The cost of living, high unemployment and poor living and working conditions made Socialists and trade unionists believe that Italy required a social revolution. Strikes and civil unrest inspired by these two organisations plagued the country, and the years 1919–20 became known as the *Bienno Rosso* (the two Red years). Landowners, industrialists, the middle class and nationalists all feared a Red revolution.

The Liberal governments of the period seemed incapable of effective action. Vittorio Orlando was blamed for the 'mutilated peace' at the end of the war, and was forced to resign in June 1919. He was followed by a succession of prime ministers — four over the next 3 years — who lacked the drive and authority to deal with Italy's social and economic problems.

How did Mussolini become prime minister?

Mussolini and the Fascists used the social and economic crisis, as well as D'Annunzio's occupation of Fiume, to their own advantage. They portrayed themselves as the only force in Italy capable of standing up to the threat of Red revolution. Fascists formed themselves into *squadristi* and these squads attacked Socialist newspapers and disrupted Socialist and trade union meetings.

The climax of the *Bienno Rosso* came in August 1920, when Socialists and trade unionists occupied factories across northern Italy. The weak Liberal government seemed incapable of stopping the unrest. The Fascists, appearing as the defenders of law and order, were seen as the only alternative. Ironically, it was not in the towns and cities that the Fascists first made their political breakthrough. By 1920, *Federterra* (Socialist peasant leagues) had appeared across northern and central Italy, and the Fascist squads who stood up to them in these areas began to gain widespread support. Mussolini could claim that, not only was he the defender of Italy against Red revolution, but also that he was prepared to use violence against his opponents in order to achieve his ends — a stance that became increasingly popular. In the national elections of May 1921, the Fascists won 35 seats — including one for Mussolini — establishing them as a major political force across northern and central Italy. On this occasion the prime minister, Giolitti, offered the Fascists a place in government, but Mussolini refused.

Mussolini's rise to power was then aided greatly by the accession to power of **Luigi Facta**, who became prime minister in February 1922. Facta proved to be a weak leader, incapable of stopping the violence between the Fascists and Socialists. In August 1922, the trade union movement called a general strike, which was broken up by Fascist squads.

In October 1922, Mussolini made his major move. The Fascists held a mass meeting in Naples on 24 October, where Mussolini declared that he would march on Rome and claim political power. On the night of 27 October, Fascists gathered in four points around Rome and occupied telephone exchanges and government offices across northern Italy. Facta was faced with a crisis; what was he to do? At 2 a.m. on 28 October, he asked **King Victor Emmanuel III** to impose martial law and send the army to arrest the Fascist leadership, to which the king agreed. However, by 9 a.m. he had changed his mind. Facta resigned as a result, and the king called on Antonio Salandra to form a government that was to include the Fascists. Once again, however, Mussolini declined. On 29 October, on the advice of Giolitti, the king asked Mussolini to be the prime minister of a coalition government of Fascists, Conservatives and Nationalists. As his five predecessors had each served for no longer than one and a half years, many felt that Mussolini's rule would be short-lived. Indeed, his actions during the 'march on Rome' would seem to have confirmed this view; instead of leading the Fascist onslaught, he had stayed in Milan with a rail ticket for Switzerland in his pocket, just in case the march on Rome backfired.

So why did the king change his mind on the morning of 28 October? One view is that he was visited between 2 a.m. and 9 a.m. by Generals Diaz and Pecori Giraldi. Although the generals stated that the army would do its duty in enforcing martial law, they advised the king not to put it to the test, suggesting that the Fascists had many sympathisers in the armed forces. Not only this, but the king feared that civil war may have broken out if he had stood up to the Fascists. Although, in reality, there were fewer than 30,000 Fascists involved in the march on Rome, the king had received reports of much greater numbers. With a weak prime minister, an army that had little stomach for martial law and the prospect of large numbers of Fascists entering Rome, the king backed down.

In his rise to the position of prime minister, Mussolini used two inter-connected tactics: bluff and intimidation. Although he despised parliamentary government, he gave the impression that the Fascists were a legitimate political party. He also linked this with the use of widespread violence against his opponents. However, even once he had become prime minister, Mussolini had limited power. He had been appointed by the king, who could dismiss him at any time, and the Fascists were still a minority group in a broader coalition of Conservatives and Nationalists.

1922–25: consolidation of power

Between October 1922 and 1925, Mussolini turned the parliamentary government of Italy into a Fascist dictatorship. His path to supreme political power was not easy and in the process he survived a number of assassination attempts.

The Catholic Church

An important factor in Mussolini's creation of a dictatorship was the support of the Catholic Church. In 1922, **Pius XI** became pope. He was anti-Communist and believed that Catholics should not be actively engaged in politics. He feared a social revolution led by Socialists and Communists. As for many other Italians, to him the Fascists seemed to be Italy's only hope of defeating this Red revolution, in spite of their association with violence. On 10 July 1923, the Pope forced the leader of the Catholic *Popolari* Party, a priest called Dom Luigi Sturzo, to resign, thus effectively removing Catholic political opposition. Mussolini also wooed Catholics with reforms, which included ordering Catholic religious instruction in all state-run schools, banning obscene publications and contraceptives and increasing the wages of Catholic priests, which were paid by the Italian state.

Fascist relations with other political parties

Mussolini received tacit support from other parliamentary politicians. On 16 November 1922, he asked parliament for extra political powers in order to deal with the political and economic crisis facing the country. His proposal was supported by five former prime ministers and passed by 368 votes to 26. In February 1923, Mussolini engineered the merger of the Fascists and nationalists under his leadership. From this year onwards, he portrayed himself as a fervent Nationalist, hoping to make Italy 'great, respected and feared' across the world.

At the Lausanne International Conference of 1923, which met to end the Greek–Turkish War, Mussolini played a prominent role. In August 1923, he ordered the Italian armed forces to occupy the Greek island of Corfu, following the assassination of an Italian general, Tellini, and four of his officers on the Greek side of the Greek–Albanian border. Although Mussolini ended the occupation following a conference of ambassadors of European states, Italy received 50 million lire in compensation from the Greek government, which Mussolini blamed for the murders. This episode showed that Mussolini was willing to be active and decisive in international affairs.

The Acerbo Law, July 1923

Mussolini's control over parliament was enhanced greatly by the passage of a new electoral law, the Acerbo Law, which he claimed was required to ensure greater political stability. Under the law, any political party gaining one quarter of the votes cast in an election would receive two thirds of the parliamentary seats. This law was passed with support from other political parties, most notably the Liberals. In the 1924 national elections, Mussolini used Fascist violence to ensure that his party would achieve a majority. Through the operation of the Acerbo Law, the Fascists gained 374 seats compared to the 180 seats gained by the opposition parties (mostly Socialists and Communists).

The Matteotti Affair and the Aventine Secession

Although Mussolini greatly increased his parliamentary base in 1924, he also almost fell from office. This occurred as a result of the Matteotti Affair. **Giacomo Matteotti** was a Socialist parliamentary deputy who was an outspoken opponent of Mussolini and the Fascists. His constant attacks on Mussolini were a cause of embarrassment. On 10 June 1923, Matteotti was murdered by a Fascist gang. Mussolini declared his innocence, but prevented parliament from meeting to discuss the murder. As a result, *Popolari*, Liberal, Socialist and Communist deputies seceded from (left) parliament in protest. This 'Aventine Secession' left the Fascists virtually in complete control of parliament. Mussolini could have been dismissed as prime minister by the king, but Victor Emmanuel did nothing. On 3 January 1925, Mussolini announced to a parliament packed with his own supporters that he took full responsibility for the Matteotti Affair. In the Senate, only 21 out of 398 senators voted against him. The vote was a vote of no confidence in Mussolini and its defeat allowed him to stay on as prime minister. From 1925, Italy was effectively a Fascist dictatorship. In September 1928, Mussolini changed the electoral law again, giving the Fascist Grand Council control over the composition of parliament.

Glossary

the Romagna: a province of northeast Italy, the capital of which is Bologna. Until 1860, it was one of the Papal States.

Paris Peace Conference of 1919–20: the conference was a meeting of the Allied powers to draw up peace treaties with the defeated central powers after the First World War. The Treaty of Versailles (1919) was with Germany; the Treaty of St Germain (1919) was with Austria; the Treaty of Trianon (1920) was with Hungary; the Treaty of Neuilly (1919) was with Bulgaria and the Treaty of Sèvres (1920) was with the Ottoman empire.

Key figures

Luigi Facta (1861–1930): born in the Piedmont region of northwest Italy Facta was prime minister from February to October 1922. He was dismissed briefly in July 1922 for not dealing effectively with Fascist violence, but when no one else was willing to be prime minister, he was reappointed by the king. In October 1922, he attempted to persuade the king to impose martial law against the Fascists. When the king changed his mind on this issue, Facta resigned.

King Victor Emmanuel III (1869–1947): noted as a man of small physical stature, Victor Emmanuel became king of Italy after the assassination of Umberto I in 1900. He was succeeded, briefly, by Umberto II in 1946. He was also emperor of Abyssinia (1936–41) and king of Albania (1939–43). He appointed Mussolini as prime minister in October 1922. He had the power to dismiss him, which he refused to do until July 1943, following Mussolini's expulsion from the Fascist Grand Council. In September 1943, Italy changed sides in the Second World War and began fighting with the Allies. The king supported this change.

Pius XI (1857–1939): elected Pope in February 1922. Born Achille Ratti, he developed a strong aversion to both socialism and communism. He supported Catholic aid for the poor and established Catholic Action for this purpose. He also disliked direct Catholic involvement in politics and was instrumental in the dissolution of the Italian Catholic party, the Popolari.

Giacomo Matteotti (1885–1924): born in northeast Italy in the Veneto province Matteotti studied law at Bologna University. He joined the Italian Socialist Party. Following Mussolini's appointment as prime minister in October 1922, he became an outspoken opponent of his government. On 10 June 1924, he was kidnapped by a Fascist gang and subsequently murdered. The uproar over his death almost brought down Mussolini's government.

The creation of the Fascist state

The corporate state

An important aspect of Mussolini's rule was the changes he made in economic policy, ideas acquired from Gabriele D'Annunzio's rule in Fiume in 1919–20. Mussolini always claimed that he was against class conflict between workers and employers and he created what became known as the 'corporate state'. This was meant to act as a model for economic and industrial harmony through unity in Italian society. The creation of the corporate state began in 1926, when **Giuseppe Bottai** created a ministry of corporations that controlled all aspects of economic activity under branches for industry, agriculture and commerce. In 1930, a national council of corporations drew together employer and worker organisations, which, by 1934, had been unified into a mixed corporation of workers and employers.

It was through corporations that industrial and economic harmony was to be achieved, as these businesses mediated in disputes between worker and employer. However, Mussolini was not completely even-handed in dealing with every side of the class divide. He suppressed Socialist and Catholic trade unions and, in the Rocco Law of April 1926, made strikes by unions illegal; the only workers' organisations which gained official recognition were Fascist syndicates. The statutory 8-hour day was replaced by a 9-hour day and in the following year, a Charter of Labour was introduced, which referred all labour disputes to a labour court appointed by the government. In addition, corporations had no official role in formulating economic policy. On the surface it looked as if economic power was decentralised under corporations; in reality the Fascist Party maintained strict control.

Economic policies

The return to economic protectionism and quota 90

When Mussolini came to power, Italy faced an economic crisis. There was a sizeable budget deficit and over 500,000 unemployed. From 1922 to 1925, when Mussolini finally gained political control, economic policy was mainly in the hands of a Liberal, Alberto Di Stefano. At the Ministry of Finance, he abolished price fixing of goods and placed price ceilings on rents for houses. He also reduced government expenditure. By 1925, unemployment had dropped to 125,000.

From 1925, however, Mussolini reversed these policies. Heavy tariffs were placed on the import of foreign goods such as grain, in an attempt to protect Italian agriculture. As a further act of economic nationalism, in 1927 Mussolini altered the exchange value of the lira to 90 lire to one British pound. However, this exchange rate overvalued the Italian currency, which had the effect of making Italian exports more expensive. In the late 1920s, before the Great Depression began with the Wall Street Crash in the USA (1929), the Italian economy suffered a slow growth rate as a result of Mussolini's policies.

Once the world entered the depressed economic conditions of the 1930s, Mussolini attempted to aid industry. In January 1933, he established the *Istituto per la Ricostruzione Industriale* (IRI, Institute for Industrial Reconstruction), which in many ways copied the Reconstruction Finance Corporation created by President Hoover in the USA in 1932. By providing loans for industry that banks could no longer make, the IRI helped Italian industry recover from the worst aspects of the global economic depression of the 1930s. Also, Mussolini's rearmament programme for the Italian armed forces aided the aircraft and shipbuilding industries. By 1940, Italy had one of the best equipped navies in Europe, after Britain.

Battles for grain and births

In 1925, Mussolini officially launched the 'Battle for Grain'. Italy, like Britain, was not self-sufficient in grain production. However, to encourage self-sufficiency (autarky) high import tariffs were placed on foreign imported grain and Italian farmers were encouraged to grow more. By 1940, Italy was producing 75% of its grain requirements. As part of this drive for agricultural self-sufficiency, Mussolini supported a policy of land reclamation. For the Fascist press and media, he was photographed stripped to the waist, working on land drainage schemes. One of the most significant of these schemes was the draining of the Pontine Marshes near Rome. This area had long been plagued by flooding and malaria, and draining it was one of Mussolini's great achievements. However, thousands of hectares of new farmland were lost as a result of the Allied invasion of Italy from 1943 to 1945.

Mussolini's campaign to increase the Italian population — the 'Battle for Births' — was rather less successful. Italy had suffered high casualties in the First World War, with 650,000 people killed. To ensure that the country would become one of Europe's major powers, it had to have a high population. As a result, large families received tax breaks while bachelors and maimed war veterans faced higher taxes from 1926. Contraception and abortion were outlawed, which pleased the Catholic Church. In 1921, the Italian population was 37.5 million; by 1941 this had risen to 44.4 million. However, part of the increase was due to the restrictions placed on Italian emigration to the USA from 1924.

Summary
Although Italy became more self-sufficient under Mussolini, it came at an economic cost. Between 1925 and 1940, economic growth averaged 0.8% per year, compared to an average of 3.8% during Liberal rule between 1900 and 1925. The index of real wages fell 11% between 1925 and 1938, as the cost of living rose. In the countryside, the agricultural labourers (peasantry) comprised 87% of the population but owned only 13% of the land. Compared to Britain, France and Germany, Italy had a relatively weak economy in 1940. The inability to meet the demands of war from 1940 to 1943 was an important contributory factor in Italy's defeat and Mussolini's fall from power.

Relations with the king and the Catholic Church

King Victor Emmanuel
Even though Mussolini became a dictator in 1925, Italy remained a constitutional monarchy. King Victor Emmanuel III appointed Mussolini as prime minister in October 1922 and, as with all previous Italian prime ministers, had the power to dismiss him. Indeed, he could have done so on a number of critical occasions, such as during the Matteotti Affair of 1924, but he proved to be a weak monarch, who was unwilling to confront Mussolini and the Fascists. He feared social revolution and preferred Fascist rule to the possible alternative of a Socialist and/or Communist government. The king's circle of advisers shared his view that Mussolini brought political and social stability after years of chaos, and Mussolini also ensured that he remained on good terms with the king. In the 1920s, Mussolini's Italy was held up as a beacon of progress in a period of uncertainty. Even Winston Churchill admired and praised Mussolini's rule. Following its conquest in 1936, Mussolini proclaimed Victor Emmanuel III emperor of Abyssinia.

However, relations between monarch and prime minister were not always cordial. In 1938, Mussolini proclaimed himself first marshal of the Italian empire, a position without precedent in Italian politics and a development that clearly displeased the king.

Eventually, following Italian defeat in north Africa and the Allied invasion and occupation of Sicily in 1943, the king dismissed Mussolini as prime minister.

The Catholic Church

Relations between the Catholic Church and the Italian state had been strained ever since the unification of Italy in 1870. Before 1871, the Pope had been an independent ruler in control of the Papal States. Italy was also overwhelmingly Roman Catholic in religion. Pope Pius IX (1846–78) refused to recognise the new Italian kingdom and in his proclamation of 1876, *Non Expedit* (Not expedient), he advised Catholics not to participate in Italian politics. However, subsequent popes, such as Benedict XV (1914–22), took a less confrontational line. In 1919, the Pope allowed a Catholic political party to be formed, the *Popolari* or PPI.

A key figure in church/state relations was Pope Pius XI (1922–39). Before becoming Pope, Achille Ratti was papal representative in Warsaw in the re-created state of Poland. He witnessed at first hand the Russian–Polish War of 1919–21, when Communist forces attempted to overrun Catholic Poland. This gave the future Pius XI a profound dislike of communism. When Mussolini began establishing his dictatorship between 1922 and 1925, the Pope did not pose any opposition. In fact, the opposite was true. Unlike his predecessor, Pius XI disliked direct Catholic involvement in Italian politics, believing that Catholics should be involved directly in social activities instead. As a result, he established a new Catholic organisation, Catholic Action. In 1923, the Pope ordered **Dom Luigi Sturzo**, a Catholic priest, to stand down as leader of the *Popolari* Party. In 1925, Mussolini declared the *Popolari* illegal and dissolved it; the Pope did not object.

Mussolini's rule also held out many attractions for the Catholic Church. For all Fascism's anti-parliamentary views, to the Pope it was better than 'godless' socialism or communism. In addition, the education minister, Giovanni Gentile's, Education Act in 1923 made Catholic religious education compulsory in all state-run elementary (primary and junior) schools, something which previous Liberal regimes had outlawed.

The most important development in church/state relations during Mussolini's time was the **Lateran** agreements of 11 February 1929, negotiations which had begun under Mussolini's predecessors. Under the Lateran Treaty, the Pope's political independence was re-established. The Italian state gave the Pope approximately one square mile of territory within Rome, to be called the Vatican City State. This was to be an independent state, with the Pope as ruler. Today it remains the world's smallest state. The Pope also received compensation of 750 million lire in cash and 1 billion lire in government bonds for papal property that lay outside the new Vatican City State, which had been taken over by the Italian government.

The second Lateran agreement was the Concordat. This determined church/state relations within the Italian state. Catholic religious instruction in schools was extended to secondary school age, and all textbooks used in state schools were first vetted by the Catholic Church.

Mussolini received considerable political benefits from the Lateran agreements:
- First, in March 1929, he decided to hold a referendum on his government, which received overwhelming popular support.
- Second, he had now effectively linked the Catholic Church with the Fascist state, which proved to have enormous propaganda value.
- Finally, it enhanced Mussolini's position as a politician and statesman. He had brought to an end decades of tension and conflict between the Catholic Church and the Italian state.

In many ways, it was one of the last acts of the unification of Italy. The agreements also improved Mussolini's reputation in international affairs, in particular with Catholic countries.

In spite of the new harmony, however, the agreements did not entirely eradicate conflict. Occasionally, the Catholic Church disapproved of Fascist attempts to woo youth away from Catholic Action and into Fascist youth organisations. In 1931, a major rift occurred when Mussolini attempted to disband the youth section of Catholic Action and merge it with the Fascist youth movement, the *Opera Nazionale Ballila*. In retaliation, the Pope issued an encyclical (declaration), *Non Abbiamo Bisogno* (We have no need), against Mussolini's actions. The Pope even threatened to excommunicate Mussolini (remove him from the Catholic faith) if he did not back down. As a result, on 2 September 1932, Mussolini announced that the proposed merger plan was cancelled.

After 1938, church/state relations were again strained by Mussolini's treatment of the Jews. In emulation of Nazi Germany, Fascist Italy passed anti-Semitic laws. For instance, in 1938 the Ministry of Education forbade any Jewish refugees, fleeing Nazi persecution, to attend Italian schools. Mussolini also forbade Jewish refugees from settling in Italian colonial territory, such as Libya.

On 6 October 1938, the Fascist Grand Council declared that Jews were not allowed to join the armed forces or the Fascist Party. These actions brought condemnation from Catholic religious leaders such as Cardinal Shuster of Milan. However, in 1939, Pope Pius XI died and was replaced by Pope Pius XII, who was less hostile to Fascism and, as the senior Catholic leader in Germany in 1933, had signed a concordat with Adolf Hitler.

Propaganda, youth and social control

The cult of Il Duce
To maintain his dictatorship, Mussolini used a variety of methods. As a former journalist, he was aware of the importance of a strong media image. He was one of

the first twentieth-century dictators to develop the idea that he was the leader of his people. Long before Hitler came to power, Mussolini had proclaimed himself Il Duce (the Leader). He developed his fine skills as a public speaker in order to portray the idea that he was the all-knowing ruler, aware of Italy's destiny and was thus the only person to make Italy a great and respected country. 'Mussolini is always right!' became a constantly used slogan in Fascist Italy. Italians were extolled to *Obedere, Credere, Combatere*! (obey, believe, fight!). Mussolini constantly associated himself with the glories of Ancient Rome. During his rule, ancient Roman monuments, such as the Colosseum in Rome, were restored. New Fascist buildings were constructed on a grand scale, imitating Roman designs. Mussolini was a new Caesar, leading Italy to glory and a great position in the world. Fascist propaganda went out of its way to portray Il Duce as a virile, healthy, dynamic ruler. Besides the photographs of him stripped to the waist working on construction and irrigation projects, others were also published of him running and horse riding. Mussolini was the Italian 'man of action'.

To enhance the public image of Mussolini as a great and wise leader, the Fascists took control of the media. The Exceptional Decrees of 1926 began the process. They gave Mussolini considerable political power to act without the authority of parliament. These were followed in 1928 by the compulsory registration of all journalists with the Fascist Journalist Association. Such measures gave Mussolini's government effective control over who could be involved in journalism and what papers could be published. In the last instance, local Fascist administrators had the power to censor what was published.

Education and youth

The basic ideas of Fascism expressed the belief that all Italian people should be subservient to the demands of the Fascist state. To ensure that this was achieved, Mussolini's regime began to impact on every feature of society. A critical area for Fascist control was education. Mussolini's government kept strict control over the school curriculum and any teachers who criticised Mussolini or Fascist ideas were removed. Junior school children were taught not to question but to obey. The so-called Fascist values of manliness, patriotism and obedience permeated all aspects of school life.

The fascistisation of youth did not end in the classroom. Every aspect of the development of Italian youth was meant to fall under the control of the Fascist government. In April 1926, a law made it compulsory to join a youth movement. This was modelled on the Boy Scout movement, but included political indoctrination as well as outdoor activities. From the ages of four to eight, boys joined the *Figli della Lupa* (Sons of the She-wolf). The organisation's name was taken from the myth that the twin founders of Rome, Romulus and Remus, had been brought up by a she-wolf, again linking Fascism with the glories of ancient Rome. From 8–13 years old, boys progressed to the *Opera Nazionale Ballila* (youth movement) and then from 14–18 to the *Avanguardisti* (the Vanguard). This was introduced in 1937 and the best members of the *Avanguardisti* could progress to the élite *Giovani Fascisti* (Young

Fascists) until the age of 21. In October 1937, all youth movements were unified into the *Giovento Italiano del Littorio* (Italian Fascist Youth), or GIL. By 1939, approximately 8 million young Italians were in the youth movement. If these young people went on to university, they could join the *Gruppo Universitari Fascisti* (Fascist University Group). Other dictators, such as Hitler and his Nazi regime from 1933, followed Mussolini's example. A complete fascistisation was limited, however, because of the role of the Catholic Church in Italy. The church vetted textbooks in school and had its own youth branch, Catholic Action. Mussolini's attempts to merge Catholic Action with Fascist youth organisations in 1931 failed due to strong papal opposition.

Leisure and sport

Once Italians reached adulthood, the Fascist state still kept control. In May 1925, the *Dopolavaro* (For the sake of Labour) organisation was founded under the umbrella of the Fascist Party. Its activities covered virtually every aspect of leisure activity, from sporting events to radio, cinema and theatre. By the end of the 1930s, it controlled all football clubs and funded libraries, drama societies and even brass bands. Membership of *Dopolovaro* rose from 300,000 in 1926 to 3.5 million in 1939. By the time of Italy's entry into the Second World War in June 1940, the *Opera Nazionale Dopolovaro* (OND) controlled 1,227 theatres, 771 cinemas, 1,230 orchestras, 6,427 libraries and 11,500 sporting groups. It turned out to be one of the most popular aspects of Mussolini's rule, partly because these activities were in themselves apolitical and thus of limited use for Fascist indoctrination.

To enhance Fascism's virile and dynamic image, Mussolini particularly encouraged the development of sport. The most popular male team sport in Italy was football. Mussolini decided to host the second football World Cup in 1934, at which Italy became world champions. His sponsorship of football continued to bear fruit in Paris in 1938, when the Italian national team, *Il Azzurri*, retained the trophy by beating Hungary 4–2 in the final. The triumph of *Il Azzurri* was hugely popular in Italy and Mussolini reaped the rewards. In 1933, an Italian won the World Professional Boxing Championship. Primo Carnera was held up as a prime example of Italian power and manliness and portrayed as a personification of all that was great about Mussolini's Italy.

The role of women

Fascism also had a major impact on the role of women in Italian society. In the Fascist Programme of 1919, women were promised the vote and complete social equality with men. However, when Mussolini took power, his promises were not kept. To the Fascists, the prime role of women was motherhood. They would be the front line soldiers in the 'Battle of Births'. The idea of a traditional family, where the husband was the wage earner and the wife was the homemaker and mother, conformed to Catholic social teaching. Other aspects of this teaching were also followed by the Fascists, such as the ban on abortion and contraceptives. In 1933, Mussolini introduced 'Mother and Child Day' to reinforce the Fascist and Catholic ideal of the woman's role.

While boys were trained in the manly arts of fieldcraft and drill, girls were educated in the arts of homemaking, sewing, cooking and child rearing. To train girls for their role in Italian society, the Fascists created the *Piccole Italiane* (Little Female Italians) for girls aged 9–14 years. From 15 to 17, they progressed to *Giovanni Italiane* (Female Italian Youth). To help with motherhood, the government created the national organisation for child rearing, the *Opera Nazionale Maternita ed Infanzià* (OMNI).

As part of this wider Fascist plan, the Ministry of Education began restricting the number of women teachers from the end of 1922. In government appointments, preference was given to men and from 1938, a law was passed limiting the number of women in the workforce to just 10%. Even within the Fascist Party, women were kept separate. They had their own organisation, known as 'Women's Auxiliaries' (*Fasci femminilli*) and their own journals, such as the *Mother's Journal* and *Female Life*. By 1935, 400,000 women were members of the Fascist Party, compared to 2 million men.

The police state

Italy under Mussolini was a police state. He had come to power constitutionally through appointment by King Victor Emmanuel. However, he had used violence and the threat of violence to pressure and intimidate political foes.

On 3 January 1925, Mussolini announced to the Italian parliament that he had created a dictatorship (although in reality it took him 2 years to create one). On 21 November 1925, shortly after an assassination attempt on him, he reintroduced capital punishment for treason. On 26 November, all political parties had to register with the police. Any breach of this law would result in the immediate disbandment of the party. In the same month, all opposition deputies were expelled from parliament. Italy was now a one-party state.

On Christmas Eve 1925, all government officials had to take a loyalty oath to Mussolini and Il Duce also changed his official title from prime minister to head of government. This meant that he was now only answerable to the king and not to parliament. To make this role effective, in January 1926, Mussolini acquired the right to rule by decree, thereby making his own laws. On 31 January 1926, he issued a law denying Italian citizenship to anyone who disturbed public order. This law allowed him to threaten and intimidate opponents.

In December 1926, the Law for the Defence of the State created a secret police and a special court for hearing political crimes. The secret police force was the *Opera Voluntaria per la Repressione Anti-fascista* (Organisation for the Repression of Anti-fascism) or OVRA. Under the leadership of Arturo Bochinni from 1926 to 1940, OVRA hunted down political opponents of the Fascist regime. Torture, beatings and imprisonment were all used by OVRA. A particular punishment was internal exile (used by the ancient Romans) to places like the Lipari Islands, off Sicily. Compared to other inter-war forces of dictatorship, such as Nazi Germany's Gestapo and SS or the NKVD of Stalin's USSR, the OVRA in Fascist Italy was relatively mild in its treatment of opponents. Out of a population of approximately 40 million, OVRA had dealt with 13,500 cases by 1943. Some 27,700 persons were imprisoned between 1926 and 1943. Only 43 death sentences for political crimes were passed in that period, of which 22 were during the Second World War.

What was Fascism?

In the period 1922 to 1943, how far was Italy governed by Fascism and how much was it the personal rule of Mussolini? In their book, *Europe 1870–1991* (2004), T. Morris and D. Murphy state that, 'the end product of the Fascist revolution was the personalised dictatorship of Mussolini'. On the surface, this seems to be true. By 1929, Mussolini was head of government and also minister of eight out of 12 government departments. He was also head of the Fascist Grand Council and the National Council of Corporations. From 1938, he even declared himself first marshal of the Italian empire. Any trip around Italy in the mid-1930s would tend to confirm this view: every town had posters of Il Duce, school books were full of references to him and so were newspapers.

Yet Italy was a Fascist state, so what did Fascism stand for? First, it was anti-parliamentarian. Fascists thought that parliamentary government was weak and divisive, responsible, at least in part, for the weakness of Italy before 1922. By 1926, parliament had lost virtually all its power. In its place was the Fascist Grand Council, a one-party organisation over which Mussolini presided. Here was where real political power lay — to the extent that it was actually the Fascist Grand Council, in July 1943, that led the way for the eventual removal of Mussolini from power.

Fascism was also anti-Socialist and anti-Communist. Fascists disliked these two ideologies for two reasons:
- They encouraged class conflict between workers and employers.
- They were international ideologies.

Fascism, particularly after the merger with the Nationalists in 1923, became nationalist and imperialist, hoping to create a new Roman empire, with Italy as the Mediterranean's main political power. Unlike the other two, Fascism was also, at its core, a conservative ideology attempting to prevent social revolution. In that sense it was anti-modernist, supporting ideas such as the family unit.

In addition, Fascism extolled action as a virtue. The previous Liberal governments had failed to deal with Italy's profound social and economic problems; Fascism, by contrast, would actively deal with these issues. In this sense, Fascism differed markedly from Communism. Communism provided a detailed plan for establishing a Communist society. Fascism, on the other hand, had no such plans when Mussolini became prime minister in 1922. The historian, Denis Mack Smith, believes that the set of ideas that became Fascism were devised *after* the creation of Mussolini's dictatorship, in order to justify it.

Who supported Fascism?

As a result of its ideas, Fascism attracted a wide variety of support. Its initial core support came from the lower middle class — shopkeepers, small businessmen and small landowners — who were particularly concerned about the rise of Socialism and Communism. From 1923, the Fascist base was broadened to include Nationalists, large landowners and industrialists, who saw the benefits of Mussolini's anti-labour legislation. The movement also received support from the armed forces. Once in power, Mussolini began a programme of military rearmament and his foreign policy — in particular the invasion of Abyssinia — also received military approval. Finally, Mussolini was supported by many Catholics, who approved of the reintroduction of Catholic religious instruction in schools and Mussolini's support of traditional family values. They were also attracted by the Lateran agreements of 1929, which ended the long-running dispute between the Pope and the Italian state.

How authoritarian was Fascist Italy?

Although a dictatorship, Italy was not a completely centralised state and had always contained strong regional identities. The Fascist Grand Council mirrored this situation, giving considerable control and authority to Fascist local leaders, known as **Ras**. Below the *Ras* were local Fascist officials called *Podesta*. Another factor limiting central control was the role and position of the Catholic Church, which kept its autonomy throughout the Fascist period. Indeed, this was even enhanced by the Concordat of 1929. However, at the head of the state was Mussolini, who ruled through his government and the Fascist Grand Council. Using propaganda and 'divide and rule' tactics, he kept himself in power for longer than any other Italian leader in the twentieth century.

Glossary

Lateran: the church in the Vatican City where the agreements were signed.

Ras: an Ethiopian term for a regional leader.

Key figures

Giuseppe Bottai (1895–1959): born in Rome Bottai joined the Fascist Party in 1919. From 1921, he became a member of the Italian national parliament. He held a variety of posts under Mussolini, such as the first Italian governor of Addis Ababa (capital of Abyssinia), mayor of Rome and minister of education, 1936–43.

Dom Luigi Sturzo (1851–1959): born in Sicily and a Catholic priest. He was one of the founders of the Catholic Popolari Party in 1919. He supported Catholic social programmes to aid the poor and was a noted anti-Fascist. Following the Matteotti Affair, he went into exile in October 1924, first in London and then in the USA in 1940. He returned to Italy in 1946 and became a senator.

Mussolini's foreign policy: 1922–43

Mussolini's aims

According to the historian, Alexander De Grand, in his book, *Italian Fascism* (1989), when Mussolini got to power in October 1922, he had given little thought to foreign policy, having spent the previous 3 years concentrating his efforts on attacking Socialists and Communists and establishing the Fascists as a force for law and order. However, a major change occurred when the Fascists merged with the Nationalists in 1923; Mussolini took over many of the foreign policy views of this former party.

The Nationalists had been appalled by the treatment of Italy during the Paris Peace Conference of 1919–20. In the Treaty of London, May 1915, Italy was promised large areas of land within the Austro-Hungarian empire when it joined the Allied side. Instead, in the Treaty of St Germain 1919, Italy received the Trentino, South Tyrol, Trieste, Istria and a small part of the Dalmatian coast. Nationalists saw this as an affront to their country. They had also hoped that Italy would dominate the Adriatic Sea. To do so, they would have to acquire territory from the newly created states of Yugoslavia and Albania. Further afield, Nationalists wanted to extend Italy's colonial empire, which, in 1922, comprised Libya, Eritrea, Italian Somaliland in east Africa and the Dodecanese islands off Turkey.

The historian, Denis Mack Smith, believed that Mussolini wished to create a new Roman empire. To do so, Italy had to dominate not just the Adriatic but also the Mediterranean Sea. An important tool in achieving this end was the Italian navy, and during his rule, Mussolini ensured that the navy was modernised and increased in size. Several of Mussolini's aims seemed similar to those of Liberal politicians before and during the First World War, with similar ambitions to build up Italy's colonial power in Africa and elsewhere.

However, there was also a Fascist dimension to Mussolini's foreign policy, in that he hoped to export Fascism to other countries. Indeed, Fascist organisations appeared in the 1920s and 1930s across Europe. Dislike of both Liberal parliamentary government and Communism led Mussolini closer to Hitler, after Hitler's rise to power in January 1933. Mussolini also supported the Heimwehr (a right-wing paramilitary organisation) in Austria in the early 1930s, and he gave material support to Franco's regime in the Spanish Civil War. Eventually in June 1940, Mussolini decided to side with Hitler's Germany in the Second World War, once it was clear that France had been defeated by the Nazi army. Ultimately, Mussolini hoped to make Italy 'great, respected and feared'.

The Lausanne Conference, Fiume and Corfu

Mussolini's first major involvement in international affairs was to represent Italy at the Lausanne Conference of 1923. In 1920, the Treaty of Sèvres had ended the war between the Allies and Ottoman Turkey. In that treaty, Italy received a 'sphere of influence' in Asia Minor (part of modern Turkey). However, a revolution took place in Turkey that brought Kemal Ataturk to power. He aimed to reverse the territorial changes made in the Treaty of Sèvres. This led to a war between Greece and Turkey, which eventually was won by Turkey.

In the Treaty of Lausanne in July 1923, Turkey regained control of much of the territory containing Turkish-speaking people that had been lost in 1920. Although Italy lost its sphere of influence, Mussolini impressed the international community by the way he represented his country's interests.

In August 1923, the Corfu incident took place. An Italian general, Tellini, and four of his officers were murdered by terrorists on the Greek side of the Albanian-Greek border. They were part of an international commission trying to decide on the precise boundary between Greece and Albania. Mussolini blamed the Greek government for the assassinations and used the Italian navy to bombard the island of Corfu, which was then occupied by Italian troops. This was done to force the Greeks to apologise and to give Italy 50 million lire in compensation. A conference of ambassadors of major European powers met and forced Italy to withdraw, but not without the 50 million lire compensation. The episode showed that Mussolini was willing to act quickly and decisively to defend Italian interests. What is also notable was the fact that the League of Nations failed to resolve the crisis.

Mussolini was more successful in his handling of the Fiume issue. After D'Annunzio had been expelled by Italian forces in 1920, the seaport came under the administration of the League of Nations. In 1924, however, Fiume was handed over to Italy. This was Mussolini's first acquisition of territory for his new Roman empire.

Extending influence in the Adriatic region

Mussolini's aim of making the Adriatic Sea 'an Italian lake' brought him into conflict with the new kingdom of Yugoslavia, a multi-racial kingdom comprising mainly Slovenes, Croats and Serbs. The Serb ethnic group was dominant and provided the royal family, but Croat separatists were demanding a separate, independent Croatia. Mussolini attempted to destabilise this new country by supporting Croat terrorists. However, in spite of their assassination of King Peter of Yugoslavia and the French president when King Peter visited France in 1934 on a state visit, the impact of Croat terrorists on the Yugoslav state was little more than an irritant.

Mussolini's relations with Albania were more successful. This state was created out of the old Ottoman Turkish empire in 1913. In 1915, during the First World War, Italian troops had occupied parts of Albania to prevent its capture by Austria-Hungary and in 1920, Albania was again declared an independent state and joined the League of Nations. However, rival factions vied for political power. In 1924, Ahmed Zog, supported by Italian money and arms, seized power. In November of the same year,

Zog, now elevated to the position of king, signed a treaty of friendship with Italy that brought Albania under Italian economic control. In 1927, Italian officers began training the Albanian army. During the economic depression of the 1930s, Albania became more dependent on Italian loans. Eventually, in April 1939, Italian armed forces occupied Albania and Mussolini claimed it as part of the Italian empire.

In consequence, by the time Italy entered the Second World War, the country had become the dominant power in the Adriatic region. Yugoslavia had proved to be a weak and divided state and Italy had extended control into the Balkan peninsula with the acquisition of Albania. Now Mussolini eyed the prospect of gaining territory from Greece, in particular the Ionian islands, which would increase Italy's hold over entry to the Adriatic Sea. He also desired the acquisition of the British-held island of Malta, as a possible Italian naval base in the central Mediterranean.

The Abyssinian War, 1935–36

To many Italians, Mussolini's decision to invade the east African kingdom of Abyssinia was unfinished business from 1896, when Italy was beaten by Abyssinia at the Battle of Adowa. It seemed, therefore, that Mussolini's policy towards Abyssinia had a large degree of continuity with colonial policies pursued by Liberal governments in the 1890s.

However, Mussolini's war with Abyssinia can also be seen as an important departure from his previous policies. During the 1920s, he had tended to follow a less aggressive foreign and imperial policy. He participated in the Lausanne Conference of 1923 and successfully negotiated the acquisition of the port of Fiume by 1924. He also signed the **Locarno Treaties** of 1925, which allowed Germany to join the League of Nations, and the Kellogg–Briand Pact of 1928, which outlawed the use of war in international affairs. In colonial affairs, negotiation and peaceful means also worked and in 1925, Mussolini acquired Jubaland from Britain, to add to Italian Somaliland.

From the early 1930s, Mussolini adopted a more aggressive foreign policy. This was due in part to the death of his brother and adviser, Arnaldo, who had been a moderating influence. At the same time, Italy — like many other European states — was suffering the effects of the worldwide economic depression. A major foreign policy triumph was seen by Mussolini as a much-needed boost to his regime.

The immediate cause of the Abyssinian War was the Wal Wal Incident of December 1934. Wal Wal was an oasis on the borders of Abyssinia and Italian Somaliland, and troops from the two countries clashed there. Abyssinia submitted the incident for **arbitration** by the League of Nations, but Mussolini used the incident to start preparing for war. Even though negotiations were taking place between Italy and Abyssinia in the first half of 1935, Mussolini used the time to amass a large army. In October 1935, he attacked Abyssinia from Italy's colonies in Eritrea and Italian Somaliland. Although the Abyssinians put up a stiff resistance, they were no match for the modern Italian armed forces, who deployed aircraft and tanks and also used poison gas against them.

Mussolini's main concern after his invasion was not the Abyssinians, but the potential reaction of the League of Nations and powers such as Britain and France. However, despite a personal appeal by the emperor of Abyssinia for help from the League of Nations at its headquarters in Geneva, the League was only willing to impose economic sanctions on Italy, which did not include oil — vital for the Italian war effort. In addition, the USA, which was not a member of the League of Nations, continued to trade with Italy.

Another key issue was the Suez Canal. This was under Britain's control and was the direct sea route from Italy to Abyssinia. If this route could not be used, then Italian ships would have to go around southern Africa. However, Britain did not close the Suez Canal to Italian shipping, which greatly aided Mussolini. Even though Italy won the Abyssinian War relatively easily, it did not stop Italy leaving the League of Nations in 1937.

The lack of strong action by the League of Nations did not mean that no attempts were made to end the conflict. In December 1935, the foreign ministers of Britain and France attempted a secret deal with Mussolini, in a belated attempt to preserve Abyssinian independence. The so-called Hoare-Laval Pact aimed to give some Abyssinian territory to Italian controlled Eritrea and Somaliland, and also to give Italy economic rights over southern Abyssinia. This pact was an early attempt to preserve international peace through **appeasing** an aggressor. When the pact became public, it caused uproar in Britain and France. Samuel Hoare, the British foreign secretary, and Pierre Laval, his French opposite number, were both forced to resign.

Ultimately, Italy's victory in the Abyssinian War caused greater distance between Italy and the Western European democracies of Britain and France, as well as helping to move Italy closer to Nazi Germany. The acquisition of Abyssinia completed Italy's conquest of east Africa. Eritrea and Italian Somaliland were now united with Abyssinia; the king of Italy was proclaimed emperor of Ethiopia (Abyssinia) and Mussolini declared himself first marshal of Italy. From a propaganda point of view, the Abyssinian War provided Mussolini with much-needed prestige. From 1936 to 1940, he eyed the conquest of Anglo-Egyptian Sudan, whose acquisition would have united his new east African empire with Italian-controlled Libya.

Following the Abyssinian War, Mussolini drifted even further away from Britain and France and closer to Nazi Germany. In late October 1936, Mussolini signed a pact with Hitler that highlighted a new direction for Italian foreign policy and, in a speech on 1 November 1936, he called this agreement the Rome–Berlin Axis.

The Spanish Civil War, 1936–39

In July 1936, civil war broke out in Spain. In the general elections of that year, a left-wing coalition of Socialists, Communists and regionalists won a hotly contested election. In the aftermath, the Spanish army attempted a takeover of power, which sparked off armed conflict. From 1936 to 1939, the Republican government, elected in 1936, fought the Nationalists led by General Francisco Franco.

Mussolini's motives for involvement in the Spanish Civil War were varied:

- First, he held a long-term dislike of left-wing regimes, which was reinforced by the links between Spain's Republican government and the USSR (which provided military aid).
- Second, Mussolini wanted to 'export' his own style of Fascist regime across southern Europe. Already in 1936, Portugal was ruled by a right-wing authoritarian government. In addition, Mussolini supported other right-wing movements, such as the Heimwehr in Austria.
- Finally, following the Abyssinian War, Mussolini drifted even further apart from Britain and France and closer to Nazi Germany. In late October 1936, Mussolini signed a pact with Hitler which highlighted a new direction for Italian foreign policy and, in a speech on 1 November 1936, he called this agreement the Rome–Berlin Axis.

Both Italy and Germany supplied support to the Spanish Nationalists. In July 1936, German and Italian transport planes helped move Franco's armed forces from Spanish Morocco to southern Spain. During the conflict, a number of foreign states supplied troops and military equipment to both sides. The Italian contribution was the largest; over 50,000 Italian 'volunteers' served on Franco's side, supported by 600 tanks and over 700 aircraft. By early 1939, Franco had won the war. For Italy, the war cost a considerable amount of money and resulted in the loss of approximately 6,000 Italians. In his book on the Spanish Civil War, *Battle for Spain* (2006), British historian Anthony Beevor claims that the Italian contribution to Franco's side was enormous and far greater than that of Germany.

Brutal friendship: relations with Germany, 1933–39

From 1936 until his fall from power in 1943, Mussolini increasingly became associated with Nazi Germany. Initially, when Hitler came to power in 1933, relations between Italy and Germany were not strong, and matters became worse in 1934, when Austrian Nazis attempted to gain power in Austria. Mussolini felt Austria was within Italy's sphere of influence in Europe and reacted by moving troops to the Austro-Italian border at the Brenner Pass, thus helping to foil the Nazi attempt.

In 1935, Mussolini feared a rearmed Germany. In March of that year, Hitler announced the introduction of conscription (compulsory military service), which broke the terms of the Treaty of Versailles, signed between Germany and the Allies at the end of the First World War. In an attempt to organise international opposition to Hitler's announcement, Britain, France and Italy met in April 1935 at Stresa in the Italian Alps. The Stresa Declaration reaffirmed British, French and Italian commitment to the Locarno treaties of 1925, which had in turn reaffirmed the Treaty of Versailles. In addition, all three powers supported the continued independence of Austria, which Mussolini feared was threatened by Hitler's Germany.

However, German–Italian relations changed following the Italian invasion of Abyssinia in October 1935. From that time onwards, Mussolini's Italy was seen as an aggressive power by Britain and France. The Rome–Berlin Axis agreement of October 1936 recognised this change. In some ways, the growing friendship between Mussolini's Italy and Nazi Germany was inevitable. Both countries wanted to follow aggressive, expansionist foreign policies. Both were also anti-Socialist and anti-Communist. To emphasise this aspect of the relationship, in 1937, Italy, Germany and Japan signed the Anti-Comintern Pact, which was overtly anti-Communist and anti-Soviet. Finally, Fascist Italy and Nazi Germany were also similar regimes. Both were anti-democratic and were led by individuals who were hailed as the national saviours of each country. Mussolini was Il Duce (the leader), a term also used to describe Hitler (Führer is German for leader).

Initially, Mussolini saw himself as the senior partner in the relationship. Italy had rearmed earlier than Germany and, as a result, was stronger militarily in 1936–37. However, by 1939, Germany was by far the stronger military power. Mussolini also saw himself as the founder and leader of right-wing movements across Europe. He had been in power since October 1922, whereas Hitler became German chancellor only in January 1933. In several ways, Hitler borrowed from Mussolini. He had studied Mussolini's public speaking style and he also adopted the Fascist salute for the Nazi Party and German armed forces. Finally, just like Mussolini's Fascists, the German Nazis adopted military style uniforms and extolled a similar message of Nationalism and national rebirth. For Mussolini, this was the creation of a new Roman empire; for Hitler, it was the creation of the Greater German Reich. To cement the links between the two countries in military terms, both Italy and Germany aided Franco in the Spanish Civil War.

A major turning point in the Mussolini–Hitler relationship came in March 1938, when German troops occupied Austria in a forced union of Anschluss between the two states. Hitler gave Mussolini only a few hours' notice of the German invasion. With tens of thousands of Italian troops fighting in Spain or occupying Abyssinia, Mussolini was in not in a position to resist Hitler's plan. From March 1938, Hitler's Germany and Mussolini's Italy had a common border at the Brenner Pass. In September of the same year, the Sudeten Crisis erupted, when Hitler demanded the handover of German-speaking areas of western Czechoslovakia (Sudetenland) to Germany. The Czech government refused. As Czechoslovakia was allied with France and the USSR, it seemed that a European war would take place. In a series of meetings, the British prime minister, Neville Chamberlain, tried to avert war through reaching agreement with Hitler. This policy of appeasement culminated in the Munich Conference at the end of September 1938. At the conference, it was decided to hand over the Sudetenland to Germany. The Czech and Soviet governments were not invited to the conference. Instead, the agreement was made between Britain, France, Germany and Italy. Mussolini and his foreign minister, **Count Ciano**, played an important role in ensuring that Hitler achieved his objectives at the conference.

In May 1939, German–Italian relations were brought even closer with the signing of the Pact of Steel. This agreement committed both sides mutually to support the other in the event of a European war. However, when war did break out following the German invasion of Poland in September 1939, Mussolini decided to stay neutral. In many ways, this was a repetition of Italy's response to the outbreak of the First World War, when it was in alliance with Germany and Austria-Hungary but similarly decided to stay neutral. However, in May 1940 Hitler launched his **Blitzkrieg** in the West against France and the **Low Countries**. Within 6 weeks, German forces had overrun these regions. The British Expeditionary Force (BEF) was forced to evacuate from mainland Europe at Dunkirk in late May and early June. With France on the verge of defeat and British forces humiliated, Mussolini took the opportunity to enter the war on 10 June 1940.

Mussolini thought he was on the winning side. Also, with the impending defeat of Britain and France, he could realise his dream of dominating the Mediterranean Sea and occupying British colonial territory in east Africa. Unfortunately for him though, the Second World War was the cause of his downfall, not his greatest triumph.

Glossary

Locarno Treaties of 1925: treaties signed between Germany and Britain, France and Italy. Germany recognised its new western frontiers, established by the Treaty of Versailles. In the following year, Germany was admitted to the League of Nations.

arbitration: the decision to submit a dispute to a third party for resolution.

appeasing: attempting to preserve peace through giving concessions to an aggressor.

Blitzkrieg: a form of modern warfare, using massed tank formations supported by aircraft and infantry.

Low Countries: a term describing the Netherlands (Holland), Belgium and Luxembourg.

Key figure

Count Galeazzo Ciano (1903–44): born in Livorno (Leghorn) in Tuscany, Count Ciano was the son of an Italian count who had been an admiral. He was an early convert to Fascism and took part in the march on Rome in October 1922. In 1930, he married Mussolini's daughter, Edda. He held a number of important posts in Mussolini's government, such as minister of press and propaganda in 1934, and foreign minister from 1936. He attended the 1938 Munich Conference and during the Second World War, he attempted to negotiate a peace with the Western Allies. As a member of the Fascist Grand Council, he voted for the dismissal of Mussolini in July 1943. He was later captured and executed by Fascist forces in 1944, on Mussolini's orders.

The impact of the Second World War on Italy

The military situation, 1940–43

When Italy came into the Second World War, Mussolini believed the war was entering its final stages. Italian troops moved into southeastern France days before France signed a ceasefire with Germany. However, the war was far from over. Britain continued fighting and defeated a German air offensive in the Battle of Britain in July–October 1940. The Italians participated in the battle by launching one air attack. All the Italian planes were shot down by the RAF before they entered British air space.

Mussolini's main aim in 1940 was to occupy Egypt, which was technically independent but was occupied by British and Commonwealth troops. They were there to protect the Suez Canal, a vital sea route giving Britain access to India and Australia. The Italians began their offensive against Egypt on 9 September. However, the vastly outnumbered British and Commonwealth forces halted the Italian advance at Mersa Matruh, just within the Egyptian border. In December 1940, they counter-attacked, expelling the Italians from Egypt and much of Libya in a lightning campaign. The complete occupation of Libya by the Allies was halted in the spring of 1941 by the appearance of a German army, the Afrika Korps, under General Rommel. Not only did Rommel save Libya from British occupation, but his offensive retook most of the lost territory.

The Italians also had ambitions of conquest in east Africa. In 1940, the Italian commander in Abyssinia, the Duke of Aosta, controlled nearly 300,000 men. Against him were small British and Commonwealth forces in Anglo-Egyptian Sudan, British Somaliland and Kenya. In June 1940, the Italians attacked British Somaliland. However, by the end of that year, the British and Commonwealth forces went on the offensive. They overran Abyssinia and won a decisive victory against the Italians in Eritrea at the Battle of Keren in February–March 1941.

In late 1940, Mussolini also attempted to expand Italian influence in the Balkans. Using their bases in Albania, Italian forces invaded Greece on 28 October. Mussolini issued an ultimatum to the Greek dictator, Metaxas, to give in. His reply of 'No' ('Ochi' in Greek) has subsequently become the name of the Greek national day. The Greek army was poorly equipped and thought to be no match for the Italians. However, the Greeks stopped the Italian attack, counter-attacked and by the spring of 1941, had occupied one-quarter of Albania. Complete Italian defeat was prevented by the intervention of Germany, whose armed forces invaded and occupied Greece in March 1941. The diversion of German troops to Greece delayed Hitler's invasion of the USSR until 22 June 1941. Because of this, Mussolini's inept invasion of Greece helped change the course of the Second World War.

Mussolini had aimed to replace Britain as the major naval power in the Mediterranean Sea and during his rule, the Italian navy had been modernised and enlarged. However, on the night of 11–12 November 1940, the Royal Navy launched a bold offensive on the main Italian naval base at Taranto, southern Italy. Aircraft from the carrier HMS *Illustrious* launched torpedo and bomb attacks, which sank half of Italy's battleships at the cost of only two aircraft. The battle changed the naval balance of power. In March 1941, another decisive British naval victory off Cape Matapan in Greece ensured that the Royal Navy remained in complete control of the Mediterranean. The Battle of Taranto proved so effective that the Japanese naval attaché to Italy reported back to Tokyo on the tactics used. Taranto became the blueprint and inspiration for the Japanese attack on Pearl Harbor on 7 December 1941.

Although the Italians lost heavily at Taranto and Matapan, they still hoped to gain possession of the British naval base on the island of Malta, due south of Sicily. Throughout 1940 and 1941, Malta was subject to constant air raids by Italian and German bombers. So great was the bombardment that the entire population of Malta was awarded the George Cross by King George VI, the highest award for civilian gallantry in the British empire. Malta never fell and its submarine flotilla caused enormous damage to the supply route for the Italian and German armies fighting in north Africa.

In 1942, Rommel launched an offensive that took the German and Italian armies deep into Egypt and threatened the seaport of Alexandria. However, at a series of battles at El Alamein, July–November 1942, the combined forces were defeated and forced to retreat across the whole of Libya and into Tunisia. Between January and May of 1943, British and Commonwealth troops from Egypt and Libya, along with US and British troops from Algeria, overran Tunisia and captured several hundred thousand German and Italian prisoners. Mussolini's dream of a new Roman empire had come to a humiliating end.

Between July and August 1943, in Operation Husky, a combined Anglo-American force invaded Sicily and occupied Italian national territory for the first time. The ease with which the Western Allies occupied Sicily suggested that it was only a matter of time before they invaded the Italian peninsula. This subsequently began in September 1943, when the British 8th Army and US 5th Army crossed the Straits of Messina and started to force their way into Italy — an invasion that was to last until April 1945.

The Italians had been defeated on every front. Their humiliation was delayed in Libya and averted in Greece only by the intervention of their German allies. Why had the Italian forces performed so poorly? Part of the answer lay in the quality of Italian arms. Italy was the first major European power to rearm after the First World War. By 1940, much of the Italian military equipment was obsolete. However, this was not the only factor. British and Commonwealth generals such as O'Connor, Wavell, Auchinleck and Montgomery performed far better than their Italian counterparts, such as **Graziani** and **Aosta**. Under Admiral Cunningham, the British Mediterranean fleet displayed enormous skill and showed conclusively the importance of aircraft carriers in naval warfare. Italy did not possess any aircraft carriers.

The home front

Mussolini's decision to enter the war was received with mixed feelings by many Italians. The national enthusiasm that greeted Italy's decision to enter the First World War in May 1915 was lacking this time. Mussolini had taken a calculated risk. He hoped the war was in its final stages and that Italy would reap the benefits of joining the winning side.

But the country was not prepared for major war and Mussolini's attempts to achieve autarky (self-sufficiency) during the 1920s and 1930s were only partially successful. The amount of Italian-produced grain had increased by 1940, but Italy still had to import both food and raw materials. The war disrupted the importation of vital goods and foodstuffs and, in 1941, the government introduced food rationing. The bread ration was only 150 grammes per day, even lower than the USSR at the height of the war. By 1943, industrial production had fallen by 35% and agricultural production by 25%. In March 1943, a major strike about food shortages occurred in the northern industrial city of Turin — the first serious strike for 20 years. Once again, Italy was facing a huge social and economic crisis.

Mussolini's regular public speeches, a feature of the pre-war era, became rare. The defeats in Abyssinia, Greece and north Africa eroded support for his regime. In 1941, Mussolini sent Italian forces to the eastern front in support of the German invasion of the USSR, only to share in the catastrophic defeat at Stalingrad in the winter of 1942–43. The war, which Mussolini thought the Germans had won in June 1940, now turned in favour of the Allies. By the end of 1942, rumours spread that plots to overthrow Mussolini were being hatched by senior army officers, leading landowners and even Church leaders. In February 1943, Mussolini sacked a large proportion of his Cabinet, including leading Fascists such as **Grandi** and Bottai. These politicians then began to conspire against him openly. In July 1943, the Allies conquered Sicily and used the island as an air base from which to bomb Rome. Mussolini's position became precarious. On 24 July, the Fascist Grand Council met and voted to end Mussolini's personal dictatorship. The following day, King Victor Emmanuel dismissed Mussolini from power. He was arrested and replaced as prime minister by the senior army officer, **Marshal Badoglio**.

Key figures

General Rodolpho Graziani (1882–1955): born in the province of Frosinone, Graziani was the senior Italian commander involved in a pacification campaign against irregular Libyan forces, 1932–33. In 1935, he was appointed governor of Italian Somaliland. From that area, he led Italian forces in the invasion of Abyssinia in October 1935. From 1936, he was a colonial administrator in Abyssinia, where he developed a reputation for brutality. With Italy's entry into the Second World War, he was appointed Italian commander in north Africa and led the invasion of Egypt in 1940, where he was defeated by a numerically inferior British and Commonwealth force. He retired from the army in 1941 and, after the war, was put on trial for war crimes and sentenced to 19 years' imprisonment. However, he was released from prison early in 1950, when he went on to form a neo-Fascist political party.

Duke of Aosta (1898–1942): a member of the Italian royal family and became Amedeo, third Duke of Aosta, in 1932. He was educated at Eton College and Oxford University. He was a tall man, at 6 feet 6 inches, compared to his cousin King Victor Emmanuel III's height of 5 feet. He served as an artillery officer in the First World War and, in 1937, was appointed governor of Abyssinia. He was commander of the Italian forces in Abyssinia in the Second World War, where he was decisively defeated by British and Commonwealth forces. He died in March 1942 of tuberculosis and malaria, in a British prisoner of war camp in Kenya.

Dino Grandi (1895–1988): born in the Romagna, like Mussolini, he was one of the more extreme Fascists. He became a member of the Italian national parliament in 1921, foreign minister in 1929 and then ambassador to Britain, 1932–39. On 24 July 1943, Grandi led the attack on Mussolini at the Fascist Grand Council meeting. In a vote of 19 to 7, with one abstention, Mussolini was dismissed. Later that year, Grandi fled Italy, first to Spain and Portugal and then to South America.

General Pietro Badoglio (1871–1956): born in the Piedmont region of northwest Italy, he was Army Chief of Staff from 1925 and was appointed governor of Libya 1928–33. He became the Italian commander in Abyssinia in November 1936 and led the Italian invasion of Greece in 1940, which proved to be a disaster. As a result, he resigned from his post in December 1943. Following Mussolini's dismissal in July 1943, the king appointed Badoglio prime minister, in which post he negotiated the Italian ceasefire with the Allies, also leading Italy into an alliance with them against Germany by September 1943.

Questions
&
Answers

This section contains five specimen exam questions. Two specimen answers are given to each question: an A-grade and a C-grade response. All the specimen answers are the subject of detailed examiner comments, preceded by the icon *e*. These should be studied carefully because they show how and why marks are awarded or lost.

When exam papers are marked, all answers are given a level of response and then a precise numerical mark. Answers are normally marked according to five levels:

- **level 1**: 1–6 marks
- **level 2**: 7–12 marks
- **level 3**: 13–18 marks
- **level 4**: 19–24 marks
- **level 5**: 25–30 marks

Question 1

How successful was the Liberal state in dealing with the problems, at home and abroad, facing Italy before the First World War?   (30 marks)

■ ■ ■

A-grade answer

In domestic affairs, they faced a troubled economy, with major regional disparities in wealth between the north and south. In addition, Italy had been a united country for only 40 years and many Italians were still not unanimous in support of the Liberal state. In foreign affairs, Italy sought a colonial empire and a major role in European international affairs. By 1915, the Liberal state had begun to address many of these problems.

✓ The introduction is clear and focused on the demands of the question. The problems faced by Italy, at home and abroad, are summarised. A brief assessment in the final sentence directly links to the question asked.

In southern Italy, much of the population was engaged in subsistence agriculture and there were high levels of illiteracy. As a result, large numbers of Italians emigrated to the New World, most notably the USA and Argentina. Even with emigration, southern Italy suffered from high levels of poverty.

In northern Italy the economic position was different. Turin and Milan were modern industrialised cities. In the years from 1896 to the First World War, the Italian economy went through a period of rapid growth. For instance, by 1915, Turin had become an important centre of automobile manufacture. However, with the growth of industrialised cities came the growth of an industrial working class. Many members of the working class in northern and central Italy became receptive to Socialist ideas and wished to see a major redistribution of economic wealth within Italy. This brought them into direct conflict with the Liberal state, which supported low taxation and minimal government intervention in economic affairs. On the eve of the First World War, Italy was facing major social unrest in the form of demonstrations and strikes. Therefore, although Italy began to modernise and improve as an economy, this brought major social change and with it, social unrest and the rise of socialism.

✓ This third paragraph deals directly with problems faced by the Liberal state, in the period 1896–1915. Assessment is accompanied by detailed supporting evidence.

In addition to the social and economic difficulties, the Liberal state also faced major political problems. Italy had been a united state only since the 1860s. For much of the period before 1915, the right to vote was limited to the wealthy. As a result, successive governments came from the middle class, with limited understanding of the aspirations of the industrial working class and agricultural labourers. By 1896, in a bid to create an element of stability between successive governments, the *transformiso* system had been developed. This meant that governments were decided more by ministers and members of parliament than by the electorate and political parties. Such a system was criticised as corrupt, sustaining government stability at the expense of real political debate on government policy. However, in 1911, the prime minister, Giovanni Giolitti, attempted to widen support for the Liberal state by extending the right to vote to most men. The broadened political base seemed to have paid dividends, as Giolitti remained in power until 1914. Yet Italy was far away from creating the solid foundations of political stability.

☑ This paragraph sustains coverage of the problems faced by the Liberal state. It covers political issues, states the problems and supports the answer with relevant knowledge. It also deals directly with the response of the Liberal state, giving an assessment of the degree of success.

Another major domestic problem facing the Liberal state was its relations with the papacy. In 1870, the Pope lost his last territorial positions in Italy. From that time onwards, the papacy was hostile to the Liberal state. In 1876, a papal declaration stated that Roman Catholics should not participate in the political life of Italy. This was a problem, because the vast majority of Italians were Roman Catholic. By 1896, many Catholics ignored this advice and became members of parliament. In 1909, the Pope relaxed his opposition to Roman Catholics participating in Italian politics. However, by 1915, the Liberal state still faced the problem of a Papacy which wished to be politically independent but occupied buildings in the Vatican in the centre of Rome, the Italian capital.

In addition to social, economic and political difficulties, Italy also faced the problem of regional diversity. Large parts of Italy possessed populations which spoke regional dialects. Italian, as a modern language, was usually the preserve of the upper and middle classes. Some attempts had been made to create greater national unity. For instance, the Liberal state supported the development of railways. However, issues of regional diversity and illiteracy remained as obstacles to the creation of a broad support for the Liberal state.

☑ The answer highlights a range of major domestic problems, which provides a comprehensive coverage in direct relation to the question. Problems are described accurately and sufficiently, and the response of the Liberal state is clearly mentioned.

In foreign affairs, successive Italian governments hoped to make Italy an important international power. In the years before 1915, European affairs were dominated by the five great powers of Germany, Russia, Britain, Austria-Hungary and France. Italy aspired to be regarded as a great power too, but it lacked the necessary military and economic power. However, this did not mean that Italy did not play an important part in European affairs. In 1882, it formed the Triple Alliance with Germany and Austria-Hungary. This was a secret military alliance mainly aimed against France and Russia. It was renewed every 3 years by Italy until 1914.

Like most of the great powers, Italy also wished to develop an overseas colonial empire. Before 1896, Italy had acquired some colonial territory in east Africa. In 1896, it attempted to extend its colonial control over east Africa with the acquisition of the ancient kingdom of Abyssinia (modern Ethiopia), but suffered a major military defeat at the hands of the Abyssinian army at the Battle of Adowa. Although this battle was a national humiliation, it did not end Italy's desire to acquire an overseas empire. Between 1911 and 1912, Italy went to war with the Ottoman empire. Italy was victorious and acquired Libya and the Dodecanese islands from Turkey. So by 1915, Italy had expanded its colonial empire, but compared to other European states such as Britain and France, this empire was relatively small.

🖉 The answer balances domestic issues with problems associated with Italy's position in the world. It also provides an assessment of how successful the Liberal state was in meeting these issues.

Therefore, by 1915, the Liberal state had begun to deal with many of the problems facing Italy at home and abroad. The Italian economy had grown rapidly from 1896 but there were still major regional differences in wealth. Also, the Liberal state was facing a new domestic challenge — the rise of Socialism. In foreign and imperial affairs, the Liberal state played an important role in European affairs and had expanded Italy's colonial empire. However, when the First World War broke out in 1914, instead of joining its allies in the Triple Alliance, Italy remained neutral. So the Liberal state had only partially dealt with the problems facing Italy. The Italian experience of war, between 1915 and 1918, exacerbated these problems, creating a postwar crisis for the Italian state.

🖉 **This essay is clearly focused. It provides analysis accompanied by detailed and relevant supporting knowledge. The answer deals with all aspects of the question in a balanced way.**

Level 5: 30/30

■ ■ ■

C-grade answer

During the period 1896 until the First World War, Italy faced many problems, both at home and abroad.

🖉 Although the introduction is relevant, it is rather brief and does not deal in any detail with what will be discussed in the answer.

The Liberal state faced many economic problems. Italy was regarded as a backward country economically within Europe. Many Italians worked in farming and many were illiterate. Farming techniques were very basic and the Italian state found it difficult to feed its population. Due to poverty and the lack of opportunity, many Italians migrated from Italy, from 1896 up to the First World War. However, this did not remove the serious problems faced by Italian agriculture. Emigration merely reduced the problem slightly. Also, in the first years of the twentieth century, Italy faced serious social unrest with many riots, demonstrations and strikes occurring. In 1898, following a rise in food prices, the workers of Milan rioted. The government introduced martial law and, in a clash between the army and rioters, 100 rioters were killed and another 400 wounded.

⚡ The answer identifies problems faced by the Liberal state. However, some of the information provided is used only descriptively. The answer lacks clear assessment of the question.

The Liberal state was also challenged by the Catholic Church. The Pope had never reconciled himself to the loss of his political independence. The Pope disliked the fact that his headquarters, at the Vatican in Rome, were now part of Italian territory. He also dissuaded Roman Catholics from taking part in Italian politics.

Finally, the political system also lacked support from the vast majority of Italians. Widely regarded as corrupt, the Liberals lacked the political power and authority to unite the country. The most influential Italian politician, from 1896 to 1914, was Giovanni Giolitti. He was prime minister from 1903–05, 1906–09 and 1911–14. However, he had served as a minister in previous governments, most notably as minister of the interior in the 1899–1903 government. Giolitti's attempts to reform and modernise Italy became known as Giolittism. Unfortunately, many of Giolitti's reforms were attacked by both right and left. Landowners thought he was going too far. Trade unions and Socialists believed he had not been radical enough. The other major group that Giolitti attempted to bring within the Liberal state was the Catholics. Many Catholics had defied papal advice and voted and participated in elections. In 1909, the Pope allowed Catholics to stand for parliament. Relying on Catholic and moderate support, Giolitti was able to become prime minister in 1909 and again in 1911.

⚡ The paragraphs above offer relevant information. This is more detailed and there is some assessment of the problems facing the Liberal state and the ways in which it attempted to deal with them.

Like other European states, Italy also wanted its 'place in the sun'. In 1881, it had hoped to acquire Tunis in north Africa, which instead fell under French control. In the 1880s, successive Italian governments wanted to establish a strong presence in east Africa. In 1883, they acquired Eritrea as a colony, followed by Somaliland in 1885. In the 1890s, they attempted to acquire Abyssinia. This plan came to an abrupt end with the Italian defeat at the Battle of Adowa, in 1896.

Defeat at the hands of Abyssinia did not end the desire of Italian nationalists to develop an Italian empire overseas. By 1911, France had extended its control over the north African coast, adding Algeria and Morocco to its previous acquisition of Tunis. This suggests that Ottoman rule in north Africa was collapsing as a result. This encouraged Italy and in September of that year, Giolitti's government decided to go to war with the Ottoman (Turkish) empire. In a brief war, Italian forces conquered the Ottoman province of Libya in north Africa. In the peace treaty with the Ottoman empire in October 1912, Italy acquired Libya and the Dodecanese islands in the Aegean Sea.

The problems facing the Liberal state abroad are identified. However, much of the information lacks direct analysis. Where analysis does exist, it is implied.

Therefore, in the period 1896 to the outbreak of the First World War, the Liberal state faced many problems. Relations did improve with the Catholic Church and Italy began acquiring an overseas empire. However, it still had serious social and economic problems.

The answer offers detailed knowledge. It identifies problems and there are implied links to the question in several paragraphs. However, most of the assessment appears in the final paragraph.

Level 3: 18/30

Question 2

How far was Mussolini's rise to power, by October 1922, due to the weakness of his opponents? (30 marks)

■ ■ ■

A-grade answer

In October 1922, King Victor Emmanuel III appointed Mussolini prime minister of Italy. This was a remarkable event, as it was only in 1919 that Mussolini had founded the Fascist Party. In 3 short years, he rose from political obscurity to the highest political post in Italy. Part of the reason for this remarkable turn of events was the weakness of his opponents, but was it the most important reason?

💡 The introduction is clear, concise and focused on the demands of the question.

Clearly Mussolini's rise was aided by the weakness of his political opponents. In the period 1919–22, Liberal politicians failed to deal adequately with Italy's postwar problems. During this time, Italy had five prime ministers. The two before Mussolini, Bonomi and Facta, were in power for only 7 and 8 months respectively. The Liberal politicians found it difficult to rule Italy in a period of crisis. They lacked the support and leadership to cope with social and economic problems and the rise of new political parties, such as the Socialists and *Popolari*.

💡 The second paragraph deals directly with the assertion in the question, through reference to the weakness of the Liberal state's political system.

A clear example of the weakness of Liberal governments was D'Annunzio's seizure of the seaport of Fiume in 1919–20. Dissatisfied with Italy's treatment at the Paris Peace Conference of 1919, D'Annunzio defied the Allied government and seized the seaport for Italy. It took nearly 18 months to eject him, and even then, the Italian government acted only under severe pressure from the Allies. The episode showed how weak Liberal government was, compared with an individual who was willing to take decisive action.

💡 This paragraph is linked clearly with the previous paragraph and offers a valid example of the weaknesses facing Liberal governments.

In particular, Mussolini's rise was aided greatly by the accession to power of Facta, who became prime minister in February 1922. Facta proved to be a weak leader, incapable of stopping the violence between the Fascists and Socialists. In August 1922, the trade union movement called a general strike, which was broken up by Fascist squads. In addition, the Fascists' main opponents were the parties of the political left, such as the Socialists and, after 1920, the Communists. Instead of uniting together to fight the Fascists, the Socialists and Communists fought each other. This benefited Mussolini greatly, as his party now only faced a set of weak Liberal politicians and a fractured political left. By October 1922, Mussolini's Fascists seemed to the king and his advisers the only political party capable of restoring law and order to Italy and opposing the rise of the political left. As a result, the king felt he had no alternative but to allow Mussolini to head a coalition government of Fascists, Conservatives and Nationalists.

However, to see Mussolini's rise purely in terms of the weakness of his opponents is simplistic. In the years 1919–22, Italy was faced with a major postwar political and economic crisis. Many Italians were dissatisfied with their country's treatment at the Paris Peace Conference, where Italy received only part of the territory promised to it in the Treaty of London, 1915, when Italy entered the war on the Allied side. The failure of the Orlando government to gain sufficient territory for Italy undermined support for the Liberal state among Nationalists.

🗩 This paragraph offers a clear link to other factors explaining Mussolini's rise to power.

Also, the end of the war brought a major economic recession, with rising unemployment. The central and northern areas of Italy were characterised by strikes, riots and demonstrations by Socialists and Communists, demanding fundamental political and economic change. Fear of socialism and communism became widespread among Italy's business and landowning classes. It was only in these crisis conditions that the Fascist Party began to grow.

Mussolini's tactics were also an important contributory factor in explaining his rise to power. He was willing to use violence and the threat of violence to extend his political influence. He was also willing to use parliament and he portrayed himself as a conventional politician, wishing to restore law and order to Italy. Fascist squads disrupted the activities of his political opponents on the left. By the autumn of 1922, it seemed that the only thing to stand between Italy and Red revolution was Mussolini's Fascist Party, which had grown in numbers in the Italian parliament following the 1921 elections.

🗩 The answer comprises of paragraphs that offer clear assessment, supported by detailed knowledge.

Finally, the 'march on Rome' was the event that allowed Mussolini to become prime minister. Mussolini's threat that he would take over power if it were not offered to him, helped persuade the king to appoint him as prime minister. This occurred even though Facta wanted the king to impose martial law. Mussolini had cleverly portrayed himself as the only politician able to save Italy from political chaos and potential left-wing revolution.

🗩 This paragraph offers an assessment of the immediate cause of Mussolini's rise to the position of prime minister.

Therefore, the weakness of his opponents was clearly an important factor in Mussolini's rise to the position of prime minister by October 1922. However, if it were not for the postwar political and economic crisis, it would be difficult to see how the Fascist Party would have won support from the more traditional parties.

question

✐ This answer offers a clear, balanced analysis of Mussolini's rise to power, where assessment is accompanied by detailed supporting evidence.

Level 5: 27/30

■ ■ ■

C-grade answer

Between 1919 and 1922, Mussolini rose to the position of Italian prime minister. In that period, he was able to defeat his Liberal and Socialist political opponents and the weakness of his opponents was an important reason for his rise to power.

✐ This is a relevant introduction, dealing directly with the assertion in the question.

In 1919, Mussolini founded the Fascist Party. In its first year, the party performed badly and did not win one seat in the 1919 elections. Originally, he hoped the Fascists would replace the Socialists as the main party of the Italian working class. However, from the end of 1919, Mussolini changed his policies and tactics to gain political power. He became anti-Socialist and strongly Nationalist.

Mussolini attempted to rise to power in a period of major economic crisis. At the end of the First World War, Italy faced rising unemployment, as hundreds of thousands of troops returned from military service and Italian industry was no longer focused on producing for the war effort. The economic crisis led to widespread strikes, riots and demonstrations, as workers and farm labourers attempted to get higher wages and better working conditions. The rise of social unrest resulted in a breakdown of law and order, which the Liberal governments of postwar Italy found difficult to deal with. In fact, from 1919 until Mussolini's rise to power in October 1922, Italy had five prime ministers. Successive governments failed to bring order to Italy and did not develop policies that would aid Italy out of the economic crisis. This suggests that his opponents were weak because they could not deal effectively with the social and economic problems facing Italy.

✐ The information in the previous two paragraphs deals directly with the circumstances surrounding Mussolini's rise to power. It places his rise in a social and economic context. Reference to the assertion in the question is mentioned in the final sentence.

Mussolini's tactics also aided his rise to power. He organised Fascist squads to attack Socialist newspapers and trade union halls. His tactics disrupted his opponents and won the Fascists support from businessmen and landowners. The Fascists were seen by many as a party of law, order and action in the face of crisis and disorder.

Mussolini also used parliament to win support. For instance, the Fascists acted as a normal political party and fought elections. Their breakthrough came in the 1921 elections, when they won many seats. Mussolini put himself forward as the only politician who could save Italy from chaos.

By October 1922, Mussolini was in a sufficiently strong position to make a bid for power in the march on Rome. He demanded that Facta's government hand over power, threatening that otherwise thousands of Fascists would march on the capital and take it instead. Faced with a Fascist takeover of power, Facta attempted to introduce martial law. However, after initially agreeing, the king eventually refused to do so, which forced Facta to resign. The king then chose Mussolini to head a coalition government of Fascists, Nationalists and Conservatives. He feared a civil war between the Fascists and the political left, but as he also feared Red revolution, he chose the Fascists.

🖉 The answer offers a variety of factors explaining Mussolini's rise. References are made to the weakness of opponents but these references are mainly implicit.

Therefore, Mussolini's rise to power was, at least in part, due to the weakness of his opponents. Successive Liberal prime ministers, such as Facta, proved to be weak and indecisive. However, Mussolini's rise was also due to his tactics of violence and via winning support in parliament. Finally, the economic crisis facing Italy after the First World War created the climate for political change which Mussolini exploited effectively.

🖉 Most of the assessment concerning the weakness of opponents is contained in the final paragraph.

Level 4: 19/30

Question 3

How successful was Mussolini's economic policy in the years 1925–40? (30 marks)

■ ■ ■

A-grade answer

Mussolini's rise to power was due, at least in part, to the economic crisis facing Italy after the First World War. If Mussolini was to retain power, he had to bring improvement and modernisation to the Italian economy. In the years from 1925, when Mussolini created a dictatorship, until the Italian entry into the Second World War, Mussolini engaged in major economic reform. These reforms brought immense change to Italy, but was Mussolini's economic policy successful?

💡 The introduction is clear and focused directly on the question. The final sentence asks a question, which will form the basis of analysis.

Many of Mussolini's economic policies were linked to his desire to make Italy a major international power. Not only did he want to improve the economy, but he also wanted to ensure that Italy could prepare itself for a possible war. Mussolini wanted to achieve autarky, or economic self-sufficiency, where Italy would produce enough food to feed its population. From 1925, heavy tariffs were placed on the import of foreign goods such as grain, in an attempt to protect Italian agriculture. Also, as an act of economic nationalism, in 1927 Mussolini altered the exchange value of the lira, to 90 lire to one British pound. This exchange rate overvalued the Italian currency, which had the effect of making Italian exports more expensive. In the late 1920s, before the Great Depression began with the Wall Street Crash in the USA in 1929, the Italian economy suffered a slow growth rate, as a result of Mussolini's policies.

💡 This paragraph deals directly with Mussolini's aims in economic policy, which forms the platform for assessment in the answer.

However, once the world entered the great economic Depression of 1929–39, Mussolini attempted to aid industry. In January 1933, he established the Institute for Industrial Reconstruction (IRI), which provided loans for industry that banks could no longer make. In many ways, it copied the Reconstruction Finance Corporation created by President Hoover in the USA in 1932. The IRI helped Italian industry get over the worst aspects of the global economic depression of the 1930s. Also, Mussolini's rearmament programme for the Italian armed forces aided the aircraft and shipbuilding industries. By 1940, Italy had one of the best equipped navies in Europe after Britain. Therefore, Mussolini was successful in one of his main aims in economic policy.

💡 This paragraph provides detailed knowledge of Mussolini's economic policy and a valid assessment of success.

As part of his autarky policy, in 1925 Mussolini officially launched the 'Battle for Grain'. Italy, like Britain, was not self-sufficient in grain production. However, to encourage self-sufficiency, high import tariffs were placed on foreign imported grain and Italian farmers were encouraged to grow more. By 1940, Italy was producing 75% of its grain requirements. As part of this drive for agricultural self-sufficiency, Mussolini supported a policy of land reclamation. One of the most significant of these schemes was the draining of the Pontine Marshes near Rome. This area had long been plagued by flooding and malaria, and draining it was one of Mussolini's great achievements. However, thousands of hectares of new farmland were lost as a result of the Allied invasion of Italy, from 1943 to 1945.

Mussolini's campaign to increase the Italian population — the 'Battle for Births' — was rather less successful. Italy had suffered high casualties in the First World War, losing 650,000 people. To ensure that Italy became one of Europe's major powers, it had to have a high population. As a result, large families received tax breaks while bachelors and maimed war veterans faced higher taxes from 1926. Contraception and abortion were outlawed, which pleased the Catholic Church. In 1921, the Italian population was 37.5 million; by 1941 this had risen to 44.4 million. However, part of the increase was due to the restrictions placed on Italian emigration to the USA from 1924.

Therefore, in conclusion, Mussolini's economic policies were only partially successful. Although Italy became more self-sufficient under Mussolini, this came at an economic cost. Between 1925 and 1940, economic growth averaged 0.8% per year, compared to an average of 3.8% during Liberal rule between 1900 and 1925. The index of real wages fell 11% between 1925 and 1938, as the cost of living rose. Also, in the countryside, the agricultural labourers (peasantry) comprised 87% of the population but owned only 13% of the land. Compared to Britain, France and Germany, Italy was a relatively weak economy in 1940. The inability to meet the demands of war from 1940 to 1943 was an important contributory factor in Italian defeat and Mussolini's fall from power.

☑ **The answer is focused clearly on the question. Assessment of the success of Mussolini's economic policies is integrated into each paragraph, with the conclusion providing a valid and logical summary.**

Level 5: 26/30

■ ■ ■

C-grade answer

In the period 1922–43, Mussolini introduced a wide variety of economic reforms that aimed to provide his regime with stability after years of social and economic crisis. From 1922, Mussolini attempted to make Italy a self-sufficient economy in terms of food production. He also wanted to increase the size of the Italian economy, in order to provide sufficient armaments for his ambitious foreign policy in the 1930s.

☑ The introduction offers a clear link to the question. It identifies Mussolini's aims in economic policy. However, it makes no direct reference to his degree of success in meeting his aims.

When Mussolini became prime minister in October 1922, there was a sizeable budget deficit and over 500,000 unemployed. From 1922 to 1925, when Mussolini finally gained political control, economic policy was mainly in the hands of a Liberal, Alberto Di Stefano. At the Ministry of Finance, he abolished price fixing of goods and price ceilings on rents for houses. He also reduced government expenditure and by 1925, unemployment had dropped to 125,000.

☑ This paragraph offers the historical context for the start of Mussolini's period in power. However, most of the information offered is only descriptive and lacks a clear assessment.

However, from 1925, when he established his dictatorship, Mussolini reversed these policies. He abandoned a low tax strategy and introduced high import taxes (tariffs) on foreign goods. He hoped this would increase demand for Italian produced goods within Italy. In a way it was partially successful, but it did damage Italy's international trade. Another damaging move by Mussolini was the decision in 1927 to set the international exchange rate at 90 Italian lire to one British pound. This made Italian exports expensive and further affected Italy's international trade.

☑ The answer adopts a narrative/chronological approach which, although offering relevant information, lacks a clear focus for assessment. Any analysis is merely implicit.

Mussolini hoped to increase Italy's ability to feed itself through increasing grain production, which he called the 'Battle for Grain'. More land was used for grain production, which included reclaimed land from marsh areas, and Italy's grain production did rise. Yet the 'Battle for Grain' was offset by the 'Battle for Births', where Mussolini attempted to increase the size of Italy's population. The Italian population rose by almost 10 million between 1922 and 1940, which meant there were more mouths to feed.

In 1929, Italy, like the rest of the world, was affected by the worldwide economic Depression. Mussolini attempted to aid industry through the government organisation IRI, which provided loans to industry. This helped industry through the worst of the economic depression.

By the time that Italy joined the war in 1940, Mussolini had made many economic reforms. He had increased food production, reclaimed land and helped increase the size of Italy's population. However, Italy was still a relatively weak economic power compared to Britain and Germany, and so Mussolini was only partially successful in his economic policy.

☑ **The answer offers relevant information. Mussolini's aims are identified in the introduction and an attempt is made to make an assessment. However, the answer does contain some lengthy narrative/chronological sections.**

Level 3: 18/30

Question 4

How far had Mussolini created a dictatorship in Italy in the years 1925–43? (30 marks)

■ ■ ■

A-grade answer

Mussolini, along with Hitler in Germany and Stalin in the USSR, is characterised as a dictator. In January 1925, he even announced that he had created a personal dictatorship. This explains, at least in part, his longevity in office, from 1922 to 1943. However, although Mussolini despised parliamentary democracy, his dictatorship in Italy was far from absolute.

This is a clear and concise introduction, setting out the context for analysis.

In many ways Mussolini's Italy, from 1925 to 1943, had the characteristics of a dictatorship. Mussolini always despised parliamentary democracy. Even before 1925, Mussolini had deliberately used violence or the threat of violence to gain political power. The march on Rome, in October 1922, and the Matteotti affair of 1924 show how the Fascists were only nominal democrats.

Although a rather short paragraph, it places in context the parameters under which Mussolini's dictatorship was established.

From 1925 until his fall from power, Mussolini ensured that political opposition within Italy would be silenced. For instance, he used violence and the threat of violence to pressure and intimidate political foes. On 21 November 1925, shortly after an assassination attempt was made on him, he reintroduced capital punishment for treason. On 26 November of the same year, all political parties had to register with the police. Any breach of this law would result in the immediate disbandment of the party. In the same month, all opposition deputies were expelled from parliament. Italy was now a one-party state — an important characteristic of a dictatorship.

As part of the process of achieving this aim, Mussolini managed to create a police state. In December 1926, the Law for the Defence of the State created a secret police and a special court for hearing political crimes. The secret police force was the OVRA. Under the leadership of Arturo Bochinni from 1926 to 1940, OVRA hunted down political opponents of the Fascist regime. Torture, beatings and imprisonment were all used. A particular punishment was internal exile (used by the ancient Romans) to places like the Lipari Islands, off Sicily. However, the OVRA in Fascist Italy was relatively mild in its treatment of opponents compared to other inter-war forces of dictatorship, such as the Gestapo and SS of Nazi Germany or the NKVD of Stalin's USSR.

The preceding paragraphs set out clearly how Mussolini created a dictatorship. They support assessment with relevant factual knowledge.

question 4

Mussolini's dictatorship also included employees of the government. On Christmas Eve 1925, all government officials had to take a loyalty oath to him and he changed his official title from prime minister to head of government. This meant that he was now answerable only to the king and not to parliament. To make this role effective, in January 1926, Mussolini acquired the right to rule by decree, thereby making his own laws. On 31 January 1926, Mussolini issued a law denying Italian citizenship to anyone who disturbed public order. This law allowed him to threaten and intimidate opponents.

To maintain his dictatorship, Mussolini used a variety of methods. As a former journalist, he was aware of the importance of a strong media image. He was one of the first twentieth-century dictators to develop the idea that he was the leader of his people. Long before Hitler came to power, Mussolini had proclaimed himself Il Duce (the Leader). He developed his fine skills as a public speaker in order to portray the idea that he was the all-knowing ruler, one who knew Italy's destiny and the only person who could make it a great and respected country. 'Mussolini is always right!' became a constantly used slogan in Fascist Italy. To enhance the public image of Mussolini as a great and wise leader, the Fascists took control of the media. The Exceptional Decrees of 1926 began the process. This was followed, in 1928, by the compulsory registration of all journalists with the Fascist Journalist Association. These measures gave Mussolini's government effective control over who could be involved in journalism and what papers were published. In the last instance, local Fascist administrators had the power to censor what was published. Therefore, Mussolini controlled parliament, the government and the media to ensure dictatorial control.

> ✒ This is a focused section of the answer. It makes clear analytical points and there is also some brief description.

Like other inter-war dictators, Mussolini ensured support for his regime through the manipulation of education and youth. His government kept strict control over the school curriculum and any teachers critical of Mussolini or Fascist ideas were removed. Junior school children were taught not to question but to obey. Also, so-called Fascist values of manliness, patriotism and obedience permeated all aspects of school life. Outside school hours, all Italian children were meant to join a Fascist youth organisation and in April 1926, a law made it compulsory to join one of these movements. They were modelled on the Scout movement, but included political indoctrination as well as outdoor activities. From the ages of 4–8 years, boys joined the Sons of the She-wolf. Later, from 8–13 years old, boys progressed to the *Opera Nazionale Ballila* and then, from 14–18, to the Vanguard. Manipulation of education and youth ensured that Fascist propaganda created support for the regime and reinforced dictatorial control of the Italian people.

Fascist control of life was also extended to adults through the *Dopolavaro* organisation, which was founded under the umbrella of the Fascist Party. Its activities covered virtually every aspect of leisure activity, from sporting events to radio, cinema and theatre. Membership of *Dopolovaro* rose from 300,000 in 1926 to 3.5 million in 1939.

However, compared to Hitler and Stalin, Mussolini was far from being an absolute dictator. First, he had been appointed prime minister by the king in October 1922, who remained as the technical head of state throughout Mussolini's period of rule. At any time after 1922, the king could have dismissed him — and at the time of the Matteotti Affair in 1924, Mussolini did indeed fear dismissal. Eventually when Mussolini fell from power in July 1943, it was King Victor Emmanuel III who discharged him.

These paragraphs introduce the balanced aspect of the answer, by identifying where Mussolini's dictatorship was limited in a number of respects.

Second, Mussolini had to contend with the independent power and influence of the Roman Catholic Church and the Pope. Italy was an overwhelmingly Roman Catholic country and Mussolini went out of his way to keep on good terms with the Church. The Catholic Church was even allowed to vet textbooks used in Italian state schools and compulsory religious lessons also became a feature of education during his rule. In 1929, he signed the Lateran Agreements with the Pope, which gave the Pope political control over the Vatican City within Rome and also gave the Catholic Church special privileges in Italy. Pope Pius XI's support for a Catholic social organisation, called Catholic Action, also limited Fascist influence over Italian youth, as Catholic Action was an organisation outside Fascist control.

Even within the Fascist Party, Mussolini's power had limitations. Considerable authority was given to local Fascist leaders, known as *Ras*. It was these regional leaders who became disillusioned with Mussolini's rule in July 1943, and voted for his removal at the Fascist Grand Council.

Therefore, superficially, Mussolini gave the appearance of being an all-knowing, powerful dictator. Although, in many ways his regime possessed the characteristics of a dictatorship, Mussolini's personal power was limited by constitutional constraints, the Catholic Church and potential opposition within his own Fascist movement.

The answer deals directly with the question. It unites analysis with detailed supporting evidence and also offers a balanced assessment of the degree to which Mussolini established a dictatorship.

Level 5: 27/30

■ ■ ■

C-grade answer

Mussolini was ruler of Italy from the end of 1922 to July 1943. In that period, he helped create a dictatorship in Italy.

This is a rather short and undeveloped introduction.

question 4

Within a year of becoming prime minister, Mussolini made sure the Acerbo Law was passed, which helped secure a clear majority for the Fascists in parliament. This was aided by a union between the Fascist Party and the Nationalists in 1923, as well as the decision by many Socialists and Liberals to leave parliament over the Matteotti Affair, which was known as the Aventine Secession. Even before his official announcement of a dictatorship in January 1925, Mussolini had created the foundations of a dictatorship.

Mussolini also detested parliamentary government. From 1925 to 1929, he created a secret police force, the OVRA, and formed a one-party state. OVRA arrested and imprisoned political opponents and ensured that Mussolini did not face opposition to his rule. He also ensured that trade unions would not strike. Although Mussolini created political stability in Italy during the 1930s, it was done so at a cost. Therefore, the creation of OVRA helped establish a dictatorship in Italy.

🗨 The information provided is relevant and a brief assessment in relation to the question is mentioned in the final sentence.

To ensure widespread support for his regime, Mussolini had effective control of the media. Censorship made sure that stories celebrating, and not criticising, Mussolini's rule were published. As part of this process, he developed the Il Duce cult, which portrayed him as the great leader of the Italian people and the only person capable of making Italy a great, respected power.

State propaganda was an important part of Mussolini's dictatorship. This even extended to education, as the Fascists had strict control over the school curriculum. In school, children were taught that Mussolini was a great leader and that their duty was to obey his government. Outside school, they were expected to join Fascist youth organisations which, again, spread the message that Mussolini was Italy's man of destiny.

Even when Italians reached adulthood, they were expected to join the *Dopolovaro* organisation, which organised sport and leisure activities. By the late 1930s, over 3 million Italians had joined it. So, from school to adult life, the Italian population was affected by Fascist propaganda.

🗨 The information in the preceding paragraphs is used mostly descriptively, with implicit links to the question.

Therefore, Mussolini did establish a dictatorship in Italy during his rule. However, he did not have complete power. He was still subject to the authority of the king, who dismissed him in July 1943, after Italy was invaded by the Allies. Mussolini also had to contend with the power and influence of the Pope and the Catholic Church, as most Italians were Roman Catholics.

🗨 **The final paragraph makes a direct assessment of the question. The answer does have clear links to the issue under discussion. However, there are also sections that are only descriptive.**

Level 4: 19/30

Question 5

To what extent was the Abyssinian (Ethiopian) War of 1935–36 the most successful part of Mussolini's foreign policy, in the years 1922–43?   (30 marks)

■ ■ ■

A-grade answer

In 1935 and 1936, the Italian armed forces successfully invaded and conquered the east African state of Abyssinia. This event was the greatest colonial achievement of Mussolini's rule. The king of Italy was proclaimed emperor of Ethiopia (Abyssinia). It seemed that Mussolini's aim of making Italy 'great, respected and feared' had been achieved, but can the Abyssinian War really be regarded as the most successful part of his foreign policy?

🖉 The introduction places the Abyssinian War in context. The final sentence provides a
platform for subsequent discussion and analysis in the remainder of the answer.

Mussolini had planned to create a new Roman empire through the extension of Italy's colonial possessions in east Africa, to include Abyssinia. The conquest of Abyssinia would give Italy considerable control and influence over the Horn of Africa region. It would also bring to an end one of the most humiliating episodes in Italian colonial history — when the Italian invasion of Abyssinia in 1896 ended with defeat at the Battle of Adowa.

🖉 The second paragraph makes a direct link with the assertion made in the question.

The Italian victory in the Abyssinian War was also exploited effectively for propaganda purposes. Along with proclaiming the king of Italy emperor of Ethiopia (Abyssinia), Mussolini gave himself the title of first marshal of Italy. Italy was proclaimed an empire and the conquest of Abyssinia was portrayed as merely the staging post for further Italian conquests. Mussolini had designs on Anglo-Egyptian Sudan, the occupation of which would have united his east African empire with Italian-controlled Libya.

However, the Abyssinian War did have a negative impact on Italian foreign policy, in that it brought to an end the diplomatic links with Britain and France. In March 1935, Germany's unilateral decision to reintroduce compulsory military service was met by the combined opposition of Britain, France and Italy, in the form of the Stresa Front. The Abyssinian War brought this front to an abrupt end. From 1935 to 1936, Mussolini began to rely much more on links with Germany. This was shown clearly with the conclusion of the Rome–Berlin Axis agreement of 1936, and the Anti-Comintern Pact of 1937. From 1936, Italy also joined Germany in aiding Franco's Nationalists in the Spanish Civil War. The Abyssinian War was the beginning of the brutal friendship between Mussolini and Hitler, which was to lead to Italy's decision to join Germany in the Second World War.

question

🖉 The preceding paragraphs place the Abyssinian War in context, through the provision of a balanced assessment of its impact on Mussolini's foreign policy.

Although the Abyssinian War was Mussolini's greatest military triumph, other aspects of his foreign policy could be seen to be more successful. In the years 1923–28, he played a central role in European diplomacy. In 1923, he was a major player at the Lausanne Conference and in 1925, Italy was one of the principal signatories of the Locarno Treaties. In 1928, Mussolini even signed the Kellogg–Briand Pact, which outlawed the use of war in international affairs. In the same period, in 1924, he was also able to acquire Fiume for Italy through international negotiation and, in the previous year, the Corfu incident showed that Mussolini was able to act decisively in defending Italian interests. In 1926, to extend Italian influence over the Adriatic region, Italy acquired economic control over Albania. So a much more successful phase in Mussolini's foreign policy was his effective diplomacy, in the years 1923–28.

Alternatively, Mussolini's intervention in the Spanish Civil War could be regarded as a great success. Italy provided both men and war material to aid Franco's Nationalists, a contribution that was far greater than Germany's. By early 1939, Franco had won the Spanish Civil War, ensuring the creation of another right-wing dictatorship in southern Europe. Italy was also able to defeat Spanish Socialism and Communism, two left-wing groups which Mussolini opposed, throughout the period 1920–43.

🖉 The two preceding paragraphs offer a balanced assessment through providing an alternative view via reference to other aspects of Mussolini's foreign policy.

Therefore, in some way the Abyssinian War was the greatest success in foreign policy, both in terms of territory acquired and military victory obtained. However, the war alienated Britain and France and forced Mussolini into closer alliance with Hitler, an association which eventually led to Mussolini's fall from power in 1943.

🖉 **This answer offers a balanced assessment which is overtly analytical throughout.**

Level 5: 28/30

■ ■ ■

C-grade answer

To Mussolini, foreign policy was always a major area of interest. He had stated that one of his main aims was to make Italy 'great, respected and feared' in international relations. As part of this aim, his victory in the Abyssinian War was extremely important.

🖉 The introduction is focused on the issue. It states Mussolini's aims in foreign policy succinctly and makes a brief assessment of the role of the Abyssinian War, in the context of his aims.

Italy had a long tradition of interest in Abyssinia. In 1896, Italian forces had invaded Abyssinia, only to be defeated at the Battle of Adowa. In December 1934, an incident occurred on the frontier between Abyssinia and Italian Somaliland, where Abyssinian and Italian troops clashed. Even though attempts were made to resolve the dispute throughout most of 1935, in this same year Italy invaded Abyssinia and conquered the country by 1936. In doing so, Italy expanded its control over east Africa. Before the war, Italy already controlled Italian Somaliland and Eritrea. Now it was the major European power in that part of Africa.

🖉 This paragraph places the Abyssinian War in a broad historical context. It also makes an assessment of the impact of the war on Italy's position as a colonial power.

The Abyssinian War also helped Mussolini put forward the idea that he was a twentieth-century Caesar, creating a new Roman empire. The Italian media made the war seem a great military and diplomatic success. The victory was followed by Italian intervention in the Spanish Civil War, on the side of Franco's Nationalists. Italy's aid to the Nationalists was a crucial element in their victory, so that was also an important part of Mussolini's foreign policy.

🖉 This paragraph sustains the link to an assessment of the role of the Abyssinian War, in the context of Mussolini's foreign policy.

Mussolini also played an important part in the Munich Agreement of September 1938. Hitler's demand, that the German-speaking parts of western Czechoslovakia — known as the Sudetenland — should be made part of Germany, almost caused a major European war. Mussolini, along with Britain's Neville Chamberlain and France's Daladier, helped prevent war through the signing of the Munich Agreement, which ended the crisis peacefully by handing over the Sudetenland to Germany.

In conclusion, the Abyssinian War was an important victory for Mussolini in foreign policy, but there were also other aspects of his conduct of foreign affairs which were successful. However, on balance, perhaps the Abyssinian War was the most successful part of his foreign policy.

🖉 **The answer is overtly analytical. However, it is rather unbalanced with a heavy concentration on the effect of the Abyssinian War on Mussolini's foreign policy, to the detriment of other factors. Also, it concentrates on the mid-to-late 1930s period, not the whole of Mussolini's era.**

Level 4: 20/30

PHILIP ALLAN
UPDATES